MAKING MOVIE MAGIC

MAKING MOVIE MAGIC

A LIFETIME CREATING SPECIAL EFFECTS FOR JAMES BOND, HARRY POTTER, SUPERMAN & MORE

JOHN RICHARDSON

WITH GARETH OWEN

FOREWORD BY RICHARD DONNER

The History Press

First published 2019

The History Press
97 St George's Place, Cheltenham,
Gloucestershire, GL50 3QB
www.thehistorypress.co.uk

British Library Cataloguing in Publication Data.
A catalogue record for this book is available from the British Library.

ISBN 978 0 7509 9123 0

Typesetting and origination by The History Press.
Printed and bound in Turkey by Imak.

CONTENTS

FOREWORD

It was a dark and stormy night ... no, no wrong book.

It started with a desperate, relatively young director with an opportunity to direct a film, which would, could, and did change his life. That's me, Richard Donner.

Flashback to 1975. London. Shepperton Studios. A book by David Seltzer called *The Antichrist*, which became *The Omen*. I was extraordinarily privileged to have in the cast Gregory Peck. Yes, Gregory Peck, the one and only – a phenomenal actor. And I was going to have the chance to direct him in a film. Also, Lee Remick, a wonderful, special, beautiful lady, and even greater actress. David Warner, an English actor, and star of one of my favourite films, *Morgan*. Plus, a supporting cast made up of the best that English theatre had to offer.

As great as all these wonderful people were, the true star of the film was a young Englishman named John Richardson. If you haven't seen the film then you won't understand this. And if you have seen *The Omen*, then you have the same respect for John as I did, do and will always have.

The Omen had to have some spectacular special effects. But we also had to keep the audience in a sense of reality, in which all these dastardly deaths and deeds were, if you could believe it, coincidental. We had to sell that in this period, in the life of the film, all hell breaks loose for Gregory and Lee and their family. And those hellish effects were mastered and executed by John.

John's father was also a master of effects, and hence John does what he does. Often, I remember kidding him when something got tough, 'Hey, why don't you call your dad to figure it out?' He took on the toughest projects and made them so very believable. In my heart of hearts, I feel that John was one of the main reasons for the success of the film.

My relationship with John continued after *The Omen* to almost every film I did that he was available for. He took on all the effects in North America for *Superman*. Effects, the likes of which had never been seen before. By the time we got to the US from our English shoot, John had everything arranged. And all I had to do was say, 'Action.'

On top of all this, John became a very special friend. And we continue our friendship to this day. Hopefully this book will not only give the reader an insight into an unseen part of motion pictures, but also one of its many great hearts.

Richard Donner, Los Angeles

INTRODUCTION

I have been very lucky in my life and career.

I have lived and worked through what I would call the golden age of the film industry – okay, we didn't have the luxury of modern technology back in the 1960s and 1970s: walkie-talkies were large, heavy and unreliable; there weren't any mobile phones or photocopiers and CGI hadn't been heard of – but we were inventive, and despite budgets being a lot tighter, schedules shorter and reshoots very rare indeed, we also had to look after our own 'health and safety' too, and I like to think we were quite good at it all.

I was privileged to work with some of the greatest directors, actors, producers, cameramen, designers and film crews, and I was very fortunate to have the very best special effects technicians on my team. It's impossible to list them all, but they know who they are, both here in the UK, and in the USA and around the world. I am also proud to say that many of my effects crew have progressed to be very successful special effects supervisors in their own right and I'd like to think I helped them along the way a little.

Through my father, Cliff Richardson, I learned about film-making, explosives, models, engineering and all of the other myriad of jobs that come under the brief heading of 'physical effects'. He was my mentor and hero.

With my first wife Jill, I had two children: Marcus who has followed me into the effects world and still works with me today, and my beautiful daughter Dominique, who wisely decided to avoid the movie industry and find success in the outside world – I am very proud of her.

Along the way I was very fortunate to live and work with the incredibly talented Liz Moore, and although our time together was cut tragically short, I will forever remember her.

I have also been incredibly lucky to have my wonderful second wife Rosie working with me for the last thirty years, on over twenty films including some of the best Bond movies and most of the Harry Potter series; she ran the office, looked after the crews, kept the continuity on set – and kept me in check and sane at the same time!

I've made some wonderful friends too, especially Mike Turk, the best boatman in the business, and Phil Hobbs, a wonderful caterer who took over the business from his father Phil Snr and went on to produce *Full Metal Jacket* for Stanley Kubrick.

Mike holds the dubious distinction of being my best man at my first marriage and again, along with Phil, at my marriage to Rosie.

I am somewhat saddened when I look at the business today as it seems to lack the fun, the passion and the job satisfaction that we all took for granted for so long. I realise I'm so lucky and privileged to have spent a lifetime in special effects and I hope the following pages convey that.

John Richardson

CHAPTER 1

PIONEERING DAYS

I can honestly say that if it wasn't for my father, I would never have thought about embarking on a career in the film business let alone be sitting here now with an Oscar, having enjoyed over five decades working with the likes of 007, Harry Potter and Superman, and a whole roster of wonderful directors including Richard Donner, James Cameron, Chris Columbus, Richard Attenborough, Billy Wilder, Ken Russell, Fred Zinnemann, Lewis Gilbert, Ron Howard, John Glen; and producers Cubby and Barbara Broccoli, Carl Foreman, John Dark, Joseph E. Levine and David Heyman plus so very many wonderful crews in all four corners of the world.

Dad, better known as Cliff Richardson, was born in 1905 and started out in the film business in 1921 when his older brother Fred got him a job at Gaumont Studios in the Shepherd's Bush suburb of west London. The studio had opened six years earlier as the first specifically-built film facility – which underlines just how much in its infancy the movie industry in the UK was. My father was at the very centre of things at, arguably, the most exciting time in this burgeoning business.

He actually started out as a prop man when the job description was a much more general one, entailing pretty much every task you can think of, from painting a set to putting up scenery and cleaning the glass in the roof – they were making silent movies back then and the stages were basically huge glass greenhouses to ensure as much natural light as possible flooded into them; soundproofing wasn't needed. I know he also had to help run the make-up department at one point and on another occasion described how he was asked to help add some 'processes' to the photography – that fateful day marked his entry into what we now call 'special effects'.

It was on a film involving Field Marshal Kitchener's ship sinking in 1916, during the height of the First World War, and there was a small set featuring a 'cut-out' depicting a section of the sea, behind which was a 'sky' backing and they placed a model of the boat in-between the two. It was mounted on two sticks with someone below moving them along – all looking a bit like a home-made puppet theatre. Dad was underneath, lying on the floor, holding a rubber bulb full of talcum powder and at the very moment the torpedo was to hit the ship, Dad squeezed as hard as he could, blasting the smoke-like powder into the air to signify a direct hit, and an explosion. The boat then slipped down behind the sea cut-out. It was both effective and convincing, and its simplicity proved also to be its brilliance.

That was, as far as I'm aware, the beginning of special effects and model work in British movies.

I'm not quite sure whether Dad was contracted to Gaumont full-time, as he seemed to move around quite a lot between other studios such as BIP (British International Pictures) at Elstree, Worton Hall in Isleworth and later, Ealing. He may well have been 'rented out' by Gaumont as and when productions came up requiring his skills, but whatever his employment status he soon developed a unique and natural flair for this new area of film-making, becoming one of the pioneers of the profession.

Amongst the more notable productions he was involved with were Alfred Hitchcock's *The Manxman* (1929), and a big location film (maybe the first to shoot in such a far-flung part of the world?) called *Timbuctoo* (1933). Unusually for producer BIP, which had a reputation for churning out cheap and cheerful quota quickies (B-movies made specifically to adhere to the 1927 Parliament Act of ensuring a certain number of British films were screened in cinemas), they gathered enough of a budget to film in Africa. The plot centred on the main character believing Timbuktu is one of the most remote and mysterious places in the world and, after falling out with his fiancée, he decides to go and live there. Much of the story is set up as a travelogue of the African terrain, its natives and their habitats which of course would have been unknown to and unseen by audiences of the time. It sounds quite idyllic but to reach the location, Dad had to cross the Sahara Desert and in doing so contracted malaria and dysentery, which plagued his health for years afterwards.

Dad worked at Ealing Studios from 1932 to 1947 which were then being run by the great Michael Balcon. He worked on many productions including *The Next of Kin* (1942) with locations in the more pleasant and easy-to-reach St Ives in Cornwall. There were obviously explosion requirements detailed in the script as Dad stored boxes full in a garage nearby, but somehow the sea air got to the flash powder and when Dad visited the garage with the prop man one day to pick up some supplies, they noticed smoke coming from the boxes. Without hesitation, Dad pushed his colleague out and shouted, 'Run!' Moments later the whole garage went BANG and despite being tens of feet away, Dad ended up with quite bad burns and was in hospital for several weeks, enduring the so-called treatment of having olive oil poured over his burns. Fifty years later, I ended up with similar burns from flash powder and know all too well just how painful it is.

Dad remained at Ealing throughout the Second World War in a 'reserved occupation' as film-making was considered very important to the war effort, and Ealing Studios was one of the few film complexes that remained open during the hostilities, making morale-boosting and propaganda movies such as *Ships With Wings* (1941) and *The Bells Go Down* (1943) (on which Dad obtained his first screen credits) – the models they built were quite fantastic. In fact, it was at Ealing that Dad met and started working with a cameraman named Roy Kellino, who pioneered and specialised in film model work, and who was the son of W.P. Kellino, a famous film director of the silent era.

Meanwhile, I came along in 1946. My first memories are probably of Spitfires flying overhead in the late 1940s and I remember standing on West Drayton bridge in Middlesex, with my mother, watching them soar across the sky. I remember the bridge because it formed part of our regular walk to West Ealing where the Lido cinema stood in all its glory, just off the Uxbridge Road. I was particularly excited whenever we went to the Lido, none more so when late one afternoon we took our seats to watch Walt Disney's *Bambi* (1942). But there was a power cut – not uncommon in the post-war years – and after sitting in the pitch dark for an hour, not having seen a frame of film, we left for home. I was quite upset, as you'll appreciate.

Sadly the Lido was demolished in 2005 and a block of flats called Lido House stands there now.

It's funny the things you remember, sometimes just fragments of memories, such as playing on the railways sidings, watching large firework parties on the green every Guy Fawkes Night, and my father bringing his work home with him – giant rubber frogs appeared in the garden, every bit as big as me; a snow machine filling the lawn with white stuff in the middle of summer; and once, just once, a huge explosion in the conservatory at the rear of the house which blew out windows and made a real mess of Dad's hand. He'd been mixing chemicals in a pestle and mortar when, I guess, the friction became a little too much. Mum was hysterical, a condition she achieved with relative ease it must be said, and that ensured it never happened again.

My arrival coincided with a period of post-war optimism in the film industry with studios such as Pinewood, Shepperton and Elstree reopening for business, and turning out scores of films to entertain the masses – and they certainly needed some light relief after six years of conflict. Dad, being quite a canny businessman, realised his career would hold more opportunities if he could move between studios and productions – so he went freelance. He worked on a few fairly nondescript films before taking on perhaps the biggest of his early career, *Captain Hornblower*, in 1950. I remember it particularly because, as a very young boy, he often took me over to Denham Studios where they were shooting huge exterior scenes on the water tank, with the wonderful galleons in all their grandeur with massive sails raised, firing canons at each other. Once I was rowed across the tank between the vessels, and somehow managed to get a splinter down the side of my fingernail from the side of the boat; it took a very large ice cream to stop my tears.

Hornblower was made long before computers had been thought of in film production and there was no such thing as CGI or digital effects, so everything was done for real, in camera and that included making the rather sedate water in the Denham tank look like it was the high seas. How did Dad do it? Well, he acquired three Mosquito aeroplanes from the RAF – they had a few they weren't using any more! – chopped their wings off and mounted the remaining bodies on rigid frames which were firmly attached to the ground. He then employed three RAF mechanics to run the engines. Of course the planes had nowhere to go, nor any means of moving, and figuring in a bit of Newton's laws of motion, Dad knew the massive wind created by the propellers would sweep across the tank, lifting the sails of the galleons as they travelled, but although he had the huge horsepower of six engines at his command, the slightest breeze from the other direction could turn the sails inside out! He never underestimated Mother Nature, and today, even with our advanced equipment and computers, we're still at her mercy.

Although the trade was already known as special effects by this time, there weren't too many people working in the field. I remember Dad often speaking about Poppa (Percy) Day at Shepperton, who was an artist who found a niche for himself in matte painting and special photographic effects in 1919 – way ahead of my father. Essentially he painted on glass, perhaps to add extensions or foregrounds to sets, and these glass plates were placed in strategic positions in front of the camera and married up to the sets behind, in perfect perspective. Poppa Day went on to work on many huge and important films such as *Things To Come* (1936), *The Life And Death Of Colonel Blimp* (1943), *Black Narcissus* (1947) and *Anna Karenina* (1948) to name but a few. Nowadays his work would be termed more 'visual effects' rather than 'special effects'. Unlike Poppa Day, my father's talents and interests didn't lie in painting but rather in chemistry; in fact he'd always hoped I might become a chemist and encouraged me to pursue science at school. As strange as it sounds in this day and age of health and safety and terrorism alerts, if you wanted, say, nitroglycerine back in the 1940s you would literally go to the local pharmacy to buy it; it was and still is used to treat heart conditions. There must have been some restrictions eventually in what explosives chemists could sell over the counter – probably after a few idiots had blown themselves up – but Dad meanwhile became great mates with all the chemists at the big fireworks companies and was forever experimenting at home with his Bunsen burner and test tubes. It's fair to say he didn't have much of a schooling and was pretty much self-taught.

I used to love going with him to Shepperton as it usually meant lunch in the wonderful restaurant. I got to know a lot of the studio personnel who worked with Dad including Wally Veevers, Ted Samuels and Ernie Sullivan in the special effects department; Frank Burden and Bert Hern in the props; along with a vast array of carpenters, riggers, plasterers and painters. Everyone was very friendly, and the studios always seemed to have a lovely homely feel about them.

As you can imagine, the seeds had started being sown as far as my future career was concerned.

Although effects work in movies developed rapidly and became more advanced over the ensuing years, I honestly believe we had to wait until 1977 and the first *Star Wars* film for a real turning point in the industry. Up until then, our budgets were really tight and we were quite often brought in on an ad hoc basis, here and there, and sometimes we were never really consulted as part of the creative process. We had to be as inventive as possible and use every ounce of our ingenuity to achieve what the scripts and directors called for. On *The Omen* for example, made just ahead of *Star Wars,* which grossed $90 million in the USA alone, the effects budget – which covered me, my assistants, our equipment, transport and everything else – was under £25,000. For that we had to take care of a decapitation, a priest being impaled, mechanical dogs, a hanging – four or five of us did everything without a computer in sight. But thanks to George Lucas, boundaries were pushed and innovations were made possible, and the effects side of the business became an integral part of moviemaking from the script stage. Since then, it's quite customary for the special effects team to sit in on script meetings and be involved early on with the production design team, the director and even the actors.

Sadly, I don't believe that is always the case now as I hear more and more from FX (effects) supervisors that some directors will only talk to them through their one or two trusted frontmen. That is not a collaboration as I know it.

There are different branches of the effects department – from physical stage effects to visual effects, model effects, CGI effects and so much more. I quite often wonder when I look back at photographs of Dad at work, if he ever imagined he was a trailblazer for so very much of the magic we see on screen today? Despite all the huge advances and all the technology we have at our fingertips today, I still can't help but marvel at the models he built – they were so detailed and effective that I'd challenge anyone to really spot the difference on film.

The sheer delight Dad revelled in daily obviously rubbed off on me, and despite his best attempts to persuade me otherwise, my regular visits to watch him at work on some of the biggest and most brilliant film sets – and he usually ended up blowing them up – proved too much of a lure!

CHAPTER 2

A CAREER BECKONS

I was educated at Manor House School in Hanwell, west London, and fondly remember the headmaster and headmistress, Mr and Mrs Chilvers. They ensured we were taught the three Rs, but also good manners and how to behave properly. I felt they developed a very natural and happy environment to be in, and as a result I happily excelled and was able to pass the entrance exam for the John Lyon School in Harrow, where I eventually took my GCE exams.

Dad was away on film locations an awful lot during my formative years, and in 1954–55 he went on one of his longest stays away from home to Madrid, working on *Alexander The Great* (1956) with Richard Burton, Claire Bloom and Stanley Baker heading the cast. Fortunately my mother and I were able to join him out there – for three whole months. I'd been granted leave of school and for a 9-year-old that would normally be excitement enough, but I had the added bonus of air travel, on a twin-engine Elizabethan-class BEA airliner. The terminal at Heathrow Airport was nothing more than a tin Nissen hut left over from the war and that was true of the airport the first few times I flew. When I look at it now, and how it sprawls across miles of west London, I yearn for the days of easy check-in and luxury service. But I digress …

Dad allowed me to visit him on set mainly to learn my way around and watch the filming, and I took to it like a duck to water – not least when a golden-haired god named Richard Burton sat me on his horse.

Dad and Roy Whybrow wrestling with the Gordian Knot on *Alexander the Great*

Dad had also been asked to work with Warwick Films around this time, a company run by Cubby Broccoli and Irving Allen, lending his expertise to several movies including *The Red Beret* (1953) and *Zarak* (1957). Little did I realise I'd be working for Cubby Broccoli in the years ahead on the James Bond films. Whilst with Warwick, Dad was forever coming and going – Morocco, India, Trinidad and even North Wales, but sadly I couldn't swing three months off school every year.

In the early 1950s in the British film industry you could count the FX (effects) people on two hands; there was the aforementioned Wally Veevers at Shepperton Studios, George Blackwell at ABPC in Borehamwood, Frank George and Bill Warrington at Pinewood, Tommy Howard and Nobby Clark at MGM, Syd Pearson at Ealing, and Dad. Yet despite little competition, Dad was out of work for a lot of the time – not every film called for FX and there were often lulls in production which meant that there was nothing at all doing. It was a very uncertain and unpredictable career.

I remember first-hand one of these perennial quiet periods over at Pinewood, particularly in 1969, when there was almost nothing in production at one point, so the management put padlocks on the stages believing they wouldn't have to pay council rates. There's nothing more depressing than seeing a film studio empty.

I gained a bit more experience with Dad on *The Last Blitzkreig* (1959) in Holland and *The Scent of Mystery* (1960) with Peter Lawford and Peter Lorre starring, and that only served to fuel my determination that after leaving school I would follow in my dad's footsteps. I naturally asked my father if he could help and his next film was to be *Exodus* (1960) directed by Otto Preminger, where I actually ended up with three jobs, the first being in the accounts department as a very junior assistant to David 'Chalkie' White, which pleased my father no end as I could tell him how much everyone else was being paid. Secondly, I had a small acting part in the film as a kibbutz guard where Preminger directed me walking back and forth across the screen telling me to 'walk slowly and look natural' – if you don't blink you can see me in the film! – and that convinced me never to try and forge a career on that side of the camera. Thirdly, and more aptly, I assisted my father – predominantly in blowing things up.

The effects department consisted of just three of us including an assistant, Roy Whybrow, from the UK, plus a couple of local helpers brought in as and when needed. I'd grown up watching my father at work and knew all too well the dangers involved in handling explosives, so was always very careful and always did as I was told. He also told me to watch what was going on around me, as I'd learn a lot.

When we were shooting in the Port of Haifa, with the old ship, the *Exodus* coming into the harbour – bearing in mind it is supposed to be 1947 – right into frame sailed the pride of the Israeli naval fleet. The huge and shiny new warship dropped anchor in the middle of our shot. Our location manager went toddling off to the harbour master and asked him to radio the ship and explain we were filming and needed it to be moved. 'I'm not moving for a film crew,' came the curt reply back from the captain.

Upon hearing this, Mr Preminger calmly walked over to the harbour master's office and said, 'Get me Ben-Gurion (former prime minister and Israel's founding father) on the phone.'

He was perfectly calm and didn't shout or rant.

Sure enough Ben-Gurion came onto the line to speak to his friend Otto, and within half an hour the ship had gone – now that's how to achieve something, I thought.

The following year, 1961, Dad started on probably his longest and toughest shoot ever, on David Lean's *Lawrence Of Arabia*. He spent at least six months working on location in Jordan – which is the one location I'd always wished I could have gone to, living in the desert, though it wasn't to be – but when they realised the 150 camels and 450 horses needed for the charge into Aqaba couldn't all be found there, it was decided to transfer a major part of the film to Spain where they spent twelve weeks in Seville, before moving 250 miles to Almeria, and that of course meant a hiatus in filming. In fact Dad went off and worked on another film whilst waiting for them all to regroup.

I visited Almeria with my mother and was able to lend Dad a hand, especially at Cabo de Gata where they filmed the famous train crash, before the unit moved to finish off the shoot in Ouarzazate, Morocco – where facilities were said to be fairly basic and difficult. I returned a decade later on *Young Winston* (1972)and would have liked to think conditions had improved but it was all pretty rudimentary then, so goodness knows what my father had to suffer.

From beginning to end, I think Dad was on *Lawrence* for just under a year and a half. He always regarded Lean as one of the greatest film directors, though he found him a little self-indulgent, and remarked to me it wasn't unusual for Lean to come onto the set in the early morning and just sit there with his head in his hands, whilst the crew stood around waiting for his thoughts and word to start. It's one of the best films ever made though, and I doubt it will ever be bettered.

Dad was no stranger to hard taskmasters such as Lean, and a decade earlier had joined Humphrey Bogart and Katharine Hepburn to work on John Huston's production *The African Queen* (1951). It was a tough film to make and Huston had really taken it on so that he could shoot and kill an elephant in the Belgian Congo – he never caught one in his sights thankfully. Fortunately, Dad was spared that location where all the cast and crew developed galloping dysentery, that is, except for Huston and Bogart who didn't, as apparently they only drank whisky. Dad was actually mainly based at Worton Hall Studios in Isleworth, sadly long gone, and I still have a rubber mould of Humphrey Bogart that he made and cast a model of, for scenes with him steering the titular boat through the rapids. Many of the boat scenes were actually filmed on the river next to Shepperton Studios, although for close-ups of Bogart pulling it through the water, they reverted back to Worton Hall and a tank specially constructed on one of the stages. Bogart was supposed to emerge covered in leeches from one such scene, but the rubber ones Dad made did sometimes fall off his oil-slicked torso. I can still remember the real leeches that dad brought home; he fed them on fresh steak so they would fill with blood and then modelled them in plasticine, made a plaster mould and turned them out in latex rubber. The water was icy cold and the director's main concern was ensuring Bogie didn't freeze in it, so they had a constant supply of buckets full of hot water, though as they were tipped in, Jack Cardiff (the director of photography) shouted, 'That's enough – I can see the damn steam.'

Then came the close-ups of real leeches. Understandably Bogart declined to be involved, so they hired a willing body double and leeches were brought over from London Zoo – tiny little worms – which horrified the director who was expecting giant slugs.

'They swell up when they taste blood!' the zookeeper explained.

But the creatures wouldn't take a hold and kept falling off. Lots of umming and ahing went on and it was suggested that maybe they should just draw a small amount of blood?

'Hang on,' they said as they pressed needle tips into the double, 'this won't hurt,' and once little drops of blood appeared, they nurtured the creatures into taking a sip. It worked!

However disaster almost struck one night, when the giant water-tank burst and a camera crane which was standing next to it was twisted like a hairpin and the huge stage door was broken too. Luckily no one had been on set.

After Dad returned from his desert adventures on *Lawrence,* I assisted him on his next film, *The Victors* (1963)*,* a war film directed by Carl Foreman in which our FX department consisted of just five people – and we had to recreate the Second World War! Mind you, when you're 16, nothing seems impossible.

We were set on a bit of a roll with war epics, as our next production together turned out to be *The 7th Dawn* (1964) with Lewis Gilbert directing and John Dark producing and we all lived in the same hotel as the stars, William Holden, Capucine and Susannah York. There were just the two of us – me and my dad – recreating war this time, and we got on with it too: everything from burning down a village, to planes dropping bombs; those bombs exploding here, there and everywhere, with added bullet hits, rain scenes ... though credit where it's due, when we burned the village down, all the guys from the construction and prop department helped set light to it in strategic positions so as to achieve the overall engulfing effect. There's no way we'd be allowed to do that nowadays, as they'd insist on a full risk assessment report and only fully trained fire handlers on set.

I loved Lewis Gilbert. He was such a brilliant director and such a kind and considerate man. He'd always make a point of coming over to me in the mornings and saying, 'Good morning boy – how's your love life?' He'd undoubtedly heard I'd been dating the Belgian ambassador's daughter, but that's another story.

Although we filmed six-day weeks on location, we never actually worked long hours and usually wrapped by 5.30 p.m. Lewis, more often than not, would look at his watch and say, 'Time to hit the pool I think.' When Lewis disappeared early one afternoon, probably to listen to a football game on the radio, we were all left waiting on set as assistant director Jack Causey wouldn't believe us when we said we'd seen him drive off. He kept us there an hour, believing no director would ever slope off early, before finally relenting.

It was a great learning curve, and I don't just mean my love life, but rather having so much to do and get on with, including setting up bullet hits around Bill Holden, on my own – a 16-year-old lad looking after Mr William Holden's special effects and being paid £10 a week too! On another occasion we had a couple of scenes to set up in a prison, one outside the front gate and the other in the central courtyard; it was supposed to be raining, though we only had one set of 'rain gear' so set it all up, as instructed, ready to shoot the scenes out front first.

'Oh no,' came word from one of the assistant directors, 'we're going to shoot in the courtyard now.'

So we duly dismantled the equipment and hosepipes, tied them all onto ropes and then I headed up onto the roof to haul it all up above the courtyard – all on my own I should add – to reassemble, reset, and start shooting.

Word then came up to me that it was back to plan A and they were going to shoot out the front of the prison after all. Of course that meant I had to – for the third time, without shooting a single frame of film – move everything and reset.

I was obviously feeling a bit wound up and frustrated and said something rather sharp. My father looked at me and said, 'We're being paid to do a job and this is what the film industry is like – if you don't like it, fuck off home.'

I have to say, those words have stuck with me for over fifty years and could be my motto.

I had my 17th birthday on the flight home; the aircrew supplied a cake and the entire crew sang 'Happy Birthday' – great memories!

CHAPTER 3

UP AND RUNNING

Lord Jim (1965) was a fairly arduous film and an adaptation of Joseph Conrad's book which took us out to Hong Kong for several months in 1963, followed by a similar time in Cambodia – I was hardly home that year.

I particularly remember the Hong Kong location because it was whilst there that news reached us that John F. Kennedy had been assassinated. It was quite scary as the news coming through was fairly sporadic and not very detailed, so no one amongst us really knew whether foreign forces were at work or what might happen as a result. This wasn't very long after the failed American invasion of Cuba – The Bay of Pigs – so you can imagine the uncertainty about whether it might spark a war was a very real concern.

Eventually we heard a little more detail and whilst it was still shocking, I must admit to feeling relieved that it seemed to be a lone gunman rather than an act of communist Russia.

On a lighter note, one sequence filmed just off Hong Kong harbour always makes me chuckle. It involved Peter O'Toole steering a junk out to sea, along with a native; the native chappie was supposed to set fire to it and jump overboard but, yes, you've guessed it, he couldn't actually swim. All eyes turned to me and it was suggested as I was going to be on board to light the fires in any case, I may as well play the part. The make-up department made me up, gave me a sarong to wear and tied a ribbon around my head. I set fire to the front of the boat then jumped overboard and for a brief moment felt very proud of myself. I say briefly because Peter O'Toole said all he could hear was my cry of 'Oh, fuck!' as I realised what I'd launched myself into – we were in a sewage cove and I was in the middle of a mass of human excrement. Peter came around to pick me up in the boat, laughing his head off, and every time I saw him on later films, he took great delight in reminding me of the incident. I saw him once at Heathrow airport and across the crowded check-in hall, Peter shouted, 'There's Richardson. He's the only man I know that voluntarily jumped into a pile of shit.'

From Hong Kong we moved to locations in Cambodia, but somehow the production office missed the opportunity to ship ahead all of the explosives that we needed for the first scenes. Realising it would delay shooting it was decided, by the powers that be, we should go out to Green Island – an ex-military base in Hong Kong where it was all stored and with a little subterfuge remove enough of the explosive to cover that early scene. The remainder could come by sea as planned, arriving in Cambodia a few days after we were due to start filming. According to plan, as we were sailing back to Hong Kong, we disappeared below decks and removed sufficient explosives to cover the first shots and walked ashore with them in our duffel bags. It was then taken back to our workshop where it

was hidden in the fog machines that were going to fly in on a cargo plane. It was all made quite safe I must add.

On arrival in Cambodia we unpacked our equipment – including the explosive – and prepared everything for the first scenes where we blew up a boat, which all went swimmingly. Everything else then arrived by sea and we continued shooting for two months.

To keep ourselves entertained in the evenings, the studio sent out 16mm prints of movies, and I was designated the projectionist for the nightly outdoor screenings, under the star-filled sky.

It was an incredible place to be, let alone film, and we were right in the heart of the wonderful Angkor Wat temple where I shuddered to see the moat full of snakes and goodness knows what else. It didn't do much for my nerves when we'd quite often be sitting in the shade of the trees during a break, only for snakes to drop from the branches – usually kraits which are the most poisonous – and land between our legs. There was no need for laxatives!

Our director Richard Brooks was a terrific man to work with but sometimes left you wondering about his rather odd beliefs. For example, my father developed stomach problems when we landed in Cambodia and had taken a couple of days off to recover; when he returned to set, Richard saw him and immediately went over. 'Jesus Christ, Cliff, no wonder you've been ill,' and reached to Dad's top pocket where he pulled out a pencil – a yellow pencil with an eraser on the end. He broke it into four pieces, tossed it into the jungle and walked back onto the set to carry on filming.

Richard was then married to actress Jean Simmons and a couple of days later Dad saw her and said, 'Jean, Richard did this thing with my pencil ...'

'Yellow pencil with an eraser? Yes, he's deadly serious,' she replied.

There's actually a wonderful TV programme of the making of *Lord Jim* called *Do it on The Whistle* (1965)which was put together by Ludovic Kennedy who joined us on location, and it's very funny – not least because of Richard Brooks.

It's a location that also holds fond memories of another sort for me as, aged 18, I had what you might describe as a 'very informative affair' with the French manageress of our hotel who was about 35. She used to give me a key to one of the empty rooms and we'd spend the night together. We met night after night, and I was really quite exhausted by the time we headed home – but it was very educational.

One of the downsides of filming in the middle of the jungle was – and probably still is – that you don't have proper toilet facilities. It was either a bucket with a lid, or you'd wander off to find a tree. Amongst the prop men was one known for his sense of humour, and he loved practical jokes. He excused himself from set during a break and positioned himself in the undergrowth one day with a long-handled spade in hand. As an unwitting crew member ambled over to take relief, dropping his trousers and crouching down, the prop man carefully leaned across with his shovel and placed it between the chap's bum and the ground, and 'caught' what was coming out. He then carefully retracted the shovel and disappeared into the jungle just as the crew member stood up and turned to inspect his deposit – and rubbed his eyes in disbelief. By the time he returned to set, holding up his trousers, we all knew what had gone on and struggled to keep straight faces as our friend started to tell us his story about the disappearing dollop.

Skipping forward to four days ahead of our departure from Cambodia and we received word that an army captain, who had been assigned to the production to keep an eye on things for the local authorities, had queried where the explosives had come from for the initial boat-blowing scene, as there was nothing detailed on the flight inventory. It had taken him two months to work that out!

Warrants for Dad, me, our assistant Roy, and production manager René DuPont's arrest were being prepared and – we heard through the grapevine – would be served on the last day of shooting so as not to disrupt things. The production office said we should get out of town quickly and flew us up to Phnom Penh, from where we boarded an early flight out of the country the next day. I was absolutely terrified that I'd feel a hand on my shoulder at immigration, but we got out without issue. The same couldn't be said for one of our wardrobe crew – he was arrested and charged with raping one of the Cambodian wardrobe assistants, which I promise you he hadn't. He was placed under house arrest until three months later; the studio Columbia Pictures paid a huge gratuity (or bribe, if you prefer) to get him out.

There was an incident with guns whilst we were on location in the jungle. All the natives involved in the battle scenes were actually members of the country's military who had been drafted in and were all dressed up as natives. One day on set I saw one of the soldiers point a gun at the leg of one of the young girl soldiers. His sergeant, or whoever it was in command, saw it too and shouted out, in a bit of a panic, 'Don't do that! You should never point a gun at anyone.'

'Why not? It's not loaded,' the soldier replied smugly as he squeezed the trigger. It actually had a blank in the chamber and the force of the blast blew a hole in the girl's leg, right down to the bone.

So never, ever, point a gun at anyone!

Judith (1966) was directed by Daniel Mann, and all about Jewish independence in the wake of the Second World War, starring Sophia Loren, Peter Finch and Jack Hawkins.

We flew off to shoot in Nahariya in the north of Israel for five months. Most of the film took place in a kibbutz with our star Sophia Loren dressed in the shortest of shorts – she never failed to turn heads. There, we found ourselves helping to recreate huge tank battles, explosions, fires, mortar bombs, bullet hits, planes dropping bombs – everything was going on albeit with the co-operation of the military.

I learned another of my life's great lessons on this film.

We naturally had a lot of guns on set which we'd taken over with us from London, and amongst them were some Mauser automatic pistols, complete with wooden stocks which clipped on to the butt and effectively gave you a short rifle. Our local army contact guy, Schlomo Lendl, brought us in a big box of live ammunition and at lunchtimes I'd go off with a gun and some bullets for target practice. One such day I took the Mauser I'd been using, placed some tins up on a wall and aimed at them – I pulled the trigger and there was a huge bang. I must admit my hand stung a bit, but all I could wonder was, 'Why hasn't the can moved?' I then looked down at the gun and saw the barrel had blown up like a split banana.

It turned out someone had put one of the decommissioned guns back in the wrong holster, and I hadn't checked it – which I admit was my fault – and the barrel of it was of course blocked. The live round had nowhere to go and so had blown back in the chamber, igniting the three other shells in the magazine to cause one heck of a bang. Yet all I came away with was a bruised hand. I vowed then to check and double-check a gun before it was used.

Being a kosher country, the laws in Israel were very strict about what could and couldn't be eaten even though we were considered tourists; certainly no bacon rolls, and milk and meat on the same table were definitely forbidden but as they say, 'When in Rome!' One evening I asked our waitress Susie what we had just eaten, she replied in a thick Hungarian accent, 'Very good, *ja*? It was stewed lung.'

We visited all parts of Israel on our days off and one of my favourite pastimes was waterskiing in Galilee which admittedly meant getting up at 5 a.m. and driving halfway across the country in my truck to meet some of the others. We'd then ski across to the far shore – which was in fact Jordan – to the point where we were under the guns on the hillside before skiing back.

As ever, the practical jokes continued on set and one of our riggers went off somewhere for the day only to return to the hotel that night to find all his furniture, including his bed, had been moved out of his room, through the window and onto the roof of the porch over the hotel entrance. He'd obviously had a few beers and thinking nothing of it just climbed out of the window and got into bed and was still there the following morning!

Dad and I next had a rather brief sojourn on *Operation Crossbow* (1965) at MGM Studios in Borehamwood, again starring Sophia Loren. We didn't stay on the film too long as Dad got a bit fed up with the politics – Tommy Howard was in overall charge of effects at the studio at the time and they didn't really see eye to eye. Fortunately we were able to go onto another MGM film called *The Mercenaries*, also known as *Dark Of The Sun* (1968), with Jack Cardiff directing and Rod Taylor starring alongside Yvette Mimieux; but in-between both MGM films we had a short spell on *Arabesque* (1966) directed by Yvette Mimieux's husband, Stanley Donen, and again starring Sophia Loren. I remember we were filming on Crumlin Bridge in Wales, which crossed a valley a couple of hundred feet below. They had just started work to demolish the bridge and as the cranes assembled and moved across into position on the other side of the structure, the whole thing swayed from side to side which made one feel distinctly uncomfortable. I was setting up bullet hits in the main on that film, and as I was wiring them all up one day, I felt someone's chin on my shoulder – it was Sophia. She said, 'How do you do this? Is it with electrolysis?' I was so surprised at seeing this beautiful face so close to me that I probably just made a series of clucking noises through my wide-open mouth before explaining how the squibs worked. On another shot we were doing the bullet hits by firing little dust-filled gelatine capsules with an airgun and in order to place them where they needed to be, I found myself hanging off the side of the bridge – without a safety harness. I didn't think I was taking any unnecessary chances but when you're young I suppose you feel quite invincible. Anyway I found myself hanging outside the railing and between the cameraman Austin Dempster's legs, and throughout the shot all I could hear was Austin asking, 'Are you still there John? Are you okay?' as he held onto my collar with one hand and operated with the other.

I next received a call to go over to Bray Studios to do a little work on *Dracula: Prince of Darkness* (1966) which Les Bowie was supervising effects on.

I'd never used any scuba gear before, nor dived, and my first day on set was actually for the final scene which sees Dracula's demise into a pool of fresh running water covered in ice. Well, it was a tank of freezing-cold water on the backlot in a freezing cold February, and the rig on which Christopher Lee was supposed to sink into the water hadn't been cabled up properly so I ended up diving in, and under the tubular scaffolding to rig a cable to it. Talk about a baptism of fire (or ice), but actually it led me to go onto getting some proper diving training which stood me well in future films.

Help! (1965) was a terrific twelve-week assignment with the Beatles when they were at the height of their popularity. Originally entitled *Eight Arms to Hold You*, and with a bigger budget than their first film, director Richard 'Dick' Lester was able to afford to shoot in colour, and David Watkin (known as Wendy to his crew) did a masterly job in lighting it with such vibrancy. Dick rarely went more than one take on any scene which was a saving that greatly pleased the producers.

The Beatles were great fun to work with but didn't seem to be really enjoying the experience, and I had the feeling they were perhaps a little bit bored with the filming process. In fact, many was the time we'd be rigging something up on the set when we were moving on to a new scene and one of the boys would pick up a guitar and start a little jam session – it was their way of relieving the monotony. Richard Lester would then play the piano and the boys could pick up virtually any instrument close to hand and start playing. It's funny to think all this terrific music was going on around us and yet it was really treated as just background music – here I was with the most famous, the most popular and brilliant pop group of our generation and it's only really in hindsight I realise how amazing and how lucky I was to be part of their ad hoc sessions – plus I was being paid.

I'm still quite amazed to think we also shot quite a bit on Salisbury Plain with tanks and even big explosions around Stonehenge. Can you imagine that nowadays?

In one scene an arrow had to come through a window of a room where two of the Fab Four were, with a red balloon attached (supposedly full of red paint). It was my job to fire it from an arrow gun and down a wire. Just so the balloon looked right we added a little red paint inside. We had the luxury of three takes, but each time the balloon hit the curtain it burst – I think it picked up a bit of static. Unfortunately it sprayed paint everywhere each time which meant a big clean up, causing Dick to say ever after for years, 'No paint in the balloon,' whenever he saw me.

But working on a film is a great leveller – well, certainly for the majority of films I've been on – as everyone is there to do a job, and yes, some may be more famous and more highly paid than others, but ultimately it's a team effort and for the most part, everyone gets on well together. That doesn't necessarily mean friendships will last beyond the production or on the other side of the studio gates, but for a few months I can honestly say the Beatles were very much four ordinary guys … well four ordinary guys who attracted hundreds of screaming girls outside the gates at Twickenham Studios on a daily basis.

Funnily enough, I later read an interview with John Lennon where he confirmed my suspicion that they were all a bit bored:

Lennon: I realise, looking back, how advanced it [*Help!*] was. It was a precursor to the Batman 'Pow! Wow!' on TV – that kind of stuff. But [Lester] never explained it to us. Partly, maybe, because we hadn't spent a lot of time together between *A Hard Day's Night* and *Help!* and partly because we were smoking marijuana for breakfast during that period. Nobody could communicate with us, it was glazed eyes and giggling all the time. In our own world. It's like doing nothing most of the time, but still having to rise at 7 a.m., so we became bored.

Richard Lester set his sights on the UK stage musical *A Funny Thing Happened on the Way to the Forum* (1966) as his next film project. He cast Zero Mostel, Frankie Howard and Michael Crawford amongst the all-star line-up and filmed in and around Madrid, in particular Manzanares where I'd visited my father on *Alexander the Great* a decade earlier.

I remember filming a Roman chariot race there and as we were galloping around, with the cameras closely following behind, we took a corner and bumped into a whole crowd of cowboys and Indians galloping towards us – they were on another production I hasten to add – and once we separated we then found ourselves in the middle of a load of tanks filming *Battle of the Bulge*. Hard to believe I know, but the Roman Empire, the Wild West and the Second World War were all shooting at the same time within half a mile of each other at what turned out to be one of Spain's most popular film locations. It sounds bonkers, and it was.

Despite being in Spain, we actually shot French hours – namely starting at 11 a.m. each morning and shooting through until 7 p.m. – after which we'd go back to our hotels to change before hitting the town, safe in the knowledge we didn't have to be in bed until 2 a.m. and could still get eight hours sleep before work.

Nic Roeg was the second unit director, who I'd met and worked with on *Judith*. After he finished that production, he went on to *Doctor Zhivago* on which he was David Lean's lighting cameraman; however, by mutual agreement, he parted company with David after a few weeks and Freddie Young took over and won the Oscar. Anyhow, Nic was always great to work with and his camera operator Alex Thompson great fun to be around. Speaking of fun, Roy Kinnear was also cast in the film. One day I was sitting with him in his caravan when he told me he'd developed a gumboil, for which he'd been given medicinal Scotch with which to bath it – several bottles in fact. Coincidentally quite a lot of the crew seemingly developed gumboils and popped by to bathe their mouths too – and Roy was all too willing to give them the benefit of his medical advice, which seemed to consist of taking several swigs before swilling another around the mouth.

Forum was also memorable as being Buster Keaton's final film; he really wasn't terribly well and rather old. Micky Dillon – who I was sharing an apartment with – was his stunt double and through him I got to meet the great Buster who I found delightful and very unassuming. I myself did a bit of doubling – not Buster Keaton, but Phil Silvers. He had a scene with Jack Gilford in which they were dressed as a pair of vestal virgins complete with blonde wigs and had to jump out of a window high up in a building to make good their escape. Micky Dillon was the only stunt-man on set that day, so naturally Dick Lester quizzed him as to how he planned the scene.

'Well I'm going to dress as Jack ... and jump out,' he replied.

'Who is going to double Phil?' Dick asked.

'I'll do them separately,' explained Micky.

'No, I need them in the same shot,' Dick countered.

Micky looked across at me, standing idly and innocently by, and then Dick turned his head, and looked up and down at me as though measuring me up.

So, yes, I had to don a blonde wig and jump out of a window for which I was offered a £10 bonus. A little negotiation took place and I got it up to £40 – as I knew there'd be several takes. The first two takes were great but on the third I missed the boxes below and exploded a few choice words. Dick didn't need to go to a fourth take.

At the 'end of picture' party, I remember there was a big dance floor with live music playing and I was standing on the sidelines with a glass in hand chatting to Zero Mostel when he asked why I wasn't dancing.

'I'm not very good,' I replied.

'Come here,' he said, and made me stand on his feet and led me around the room. What a way to end a film!

If you thought my tale of cowboys and Indians and Second World War tanks almost appearing in the same scene was a bit far-fetched, you really should watch *Casino Royale* (1967). It was the first film I received a credit on, and what a heck of a production it was to earn that credit – sprawled across four studios, with four James Bonds and seven directors. Peter Sellers was the star, and producer Charles K. Feldman wanted him so much he agreed to his demand for a (huge) fee of $750,000. But Sellers proved highly unpredictable and was then suffering problems in his romance with Britt Ekland so would disappear for days on end.

Director Joe McGrath – who as a first-time feature director got the job because he was Peter Sellers's mate – tried to keep his star in check, but it proved increasingly difficult. Script changes were a regular occurrence and the relationship between Sellers and his co-star Orson Welles, who played villain LeChiffre, was stretched even before they met. Sellers was terrified of having to work with Welles and turned it into a resentment of the actor. It all exploded when he invited Princess Margaret to Shepperton. Welles, unbeknown to Sellers, had become a friend of the Princess some years earlier and as HRH arrived, she passed right by Sellers and went over to Orson Welles: 'Hello Orson,' she said. 'I haven't seen you for days!'

Peter Sellers went as white as a sheet and was infuriated beyond belief that Welles had upstaged him. As a consequence, Sellers insisted that all of his scenes with Welles be shot in such a way so as neither actor had to appear together. But we were shooting in widescreen and Joe McGrath said it would look 'stupid' not to have them both in the wide shots. He laid it on a bit further, having a go at Sellers over his poor timekeeping and general unprofessional attitude. The actor seemed to listen, take it in and then retired with McGrath to his trailer to discuss a scene. Rumour has it that once inside Sellers said, 'I've had enough of this,' and swung at McGrath.

McGrath swung back. Fortunately the pair were separated by stuntman Gerry Crampton.

Sellers, feeling totally embarrassed, disappeared again and let it be known he'd only come back, 'if I don't play any scenes with Orson.' Joe McGrath said, 'Get lost' and left the picture.

Robert Parrish took over from Joe, then John Huston (who also appeared in the movie and I had to whip his toupee off in an explosion) had a go, followed by Val Guest, Ken Hughes and Richard Talmadge, an old US stuntman turned director who'd probably broken just about every bone in his body. The only other director I can remember on the film was Tony Squires who did mostly location filming. With each director came new ideas and consequently the casino set, which had been constructed on a stage at Shepperton Studios for a three-week shoot (though was actually shot on for six weeks) was struck and re-built on another stage – perhaps whilst awaiting new script pages? – but was never shot on. It was struck again, only to be re-built on the large silent stage, H Stage, at the studio where they filmed on it for three months!

Incidentally, there had been a rather nice and rather huge brown carpet on the floor of the entire casino set but on the third time of building they rolled it out only to discover in the centre – where it was nice and clean – someone had cut out the shape of a living room, even the bit around a fireplace, and nicked it.

One of my first solo jobs, without Dad, was blowing up the torture chamber where Orson Welles was situated, and I'd rigged up various charges and explosions. Orson came in and I talked him through it, explaining that when he fell forward dead, he must be sure to do so 'there' – which was away from the charges. He obviously didn't listen as he put his hand out right over one of the charges as he fell, and although not injured badly he did get a nasty burn. He jumped up, shouted, 'Cut!' and then started ranting, calling me an idiot.

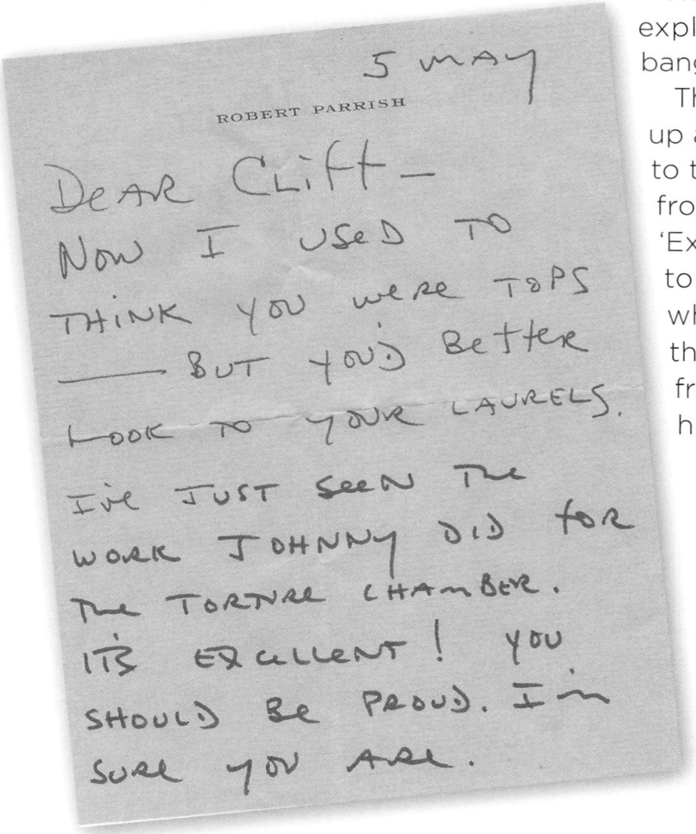

'I'm terribly sorry, sir,' I replied, 'but I did explain where to fall and where all the bangs were going to go off.'

They called for take two, so I rigged it all up again and waited for Orson to return to the set. Much to my astonishment, in front of the whole crew, he called out, 'Excuse me all. I just want to apologise to this young man as I shouted at him when in fact it wasn't his fault at all.' I thought that was pretty good coming from a star such as him and respected him hugely thereafter.

ROBERT PARRISH

5 MAY

Dear Cliff –
Now I used to think you were tops —— but you'd better look to your laurels.

I've just seen the work Johnny did for the torture chamber. It's excellent! You should be proud. I'm sure you are.

One day Jerry Bresler walked onto the set and announced himself as the new producer – new producer, new ideas: a consequence of which saw the production scrap £1 million worth of sets.

Eleven writers in all had a hand in the script, including Val Guest, John Law, Michael Sayers, Wolf Mankowitz, Ben Hecht, Peter Sellers and Woody Allen. One of the rewrites – I'm not sure whose – called for the Elgin Marbles to be used, and art director Michael Stringer was sent off to get casts from the British Museum. What with that and flying saucers appearing, it was becoming madness, and going massively over-budget and schedule. Peter Sellers decided he'd had enough and left, and that's when Terence Cooper was drafted in as yet another 007 – we already had David Niven and Woody Allen – to replace him.

John Dark, the associate producer, was someone I worked with quite a lot in later years. He told me that he'd initially been sent to Rome to set up the film, and was making all the preparations when producer Charles K. Feldman phoned him and asked what the hell he was doing in Italy as it had been decided to film in London.

Decided by whom? When?

John was later faced with stepping in when the director (at that point), Robert Talmadge, suggested to me that some of the stuntmen, dressed as Native American Indians, should fire flaming arrows into the crowd in the casino. I refused saying I wouldn't do it, as it was too dangerous. 'But the arrows have rubber tips on?' he reasoned.

'They'll be alight!' I replied bluntly.

I was summoned off the stage and to a telephone where Feldman was waiting to speak to me at the other end.

'I hear you're refusing to do what the director asks of you?'

I said, 'Yes sir, I have, because I think it's very dangerous.'

'Put John Dark back on, would you?' he asked.

That was the last I heard about the idea.

The highlight of the film for me was keeping the foam bubbles going in the bath as Ursula Andress sat in it with very little on … happy days!

It was undoubtedly the most chaotic film I've ever worked on; fortunately my father left before the end of the fifteen-month shoot because he was contracted to *The Dirty Dozen* (1967) and said my services were required too. Thank goodness.

What a cast we had with *Dozen*, including Telly Savalas, Lee Marvin, Charles Bronson and Donald Sutherland amongst others. My enduring memory is how they all loved playing poker every day around the back of the set – there were some fairly hefty stakes around that table.

With Richard Talmage the Second Unit Director on *Casino Royale*

We filmed all around the UK and then pulled back to MGM in Borehamwood on the lot and stages; blowing up the chateau at the end of the film was one of the highlights for me. MGM was a great studio, and the only really purpose-built studio in Britain of the era, with a great backlot, where you could stand and turn 360° and not see a building; great stages, fantastic workshops, but terrible management.

The gate was run by the most militant ex-traffic wardens you could ever encounter, and they wouldn't let cars in, instead sending you off to an outside car park – which was rife with car thieves as it wasn't monitored. So I used to drive in and say I had explosives in the boot for all the 'bullet hits' that we would be using on-set during the day. That always worked and they had to let me through, and I parked right outside the stage.

It was sad when after merging that studio with the Associated British (ABPC) across the road in 1970, the management ruled that it was only financially viable to keep one of the two sites open and closed the far superior MGM one. I've never been sure of the reasoning behind it and in fact would have thought ABPC would have been the more obvious choice, not only for operational reasons but because it was nearest to the high street and more valuable land for redevelopment.

Duffy (1968) was the first film I worked on, on my own, as a full FX supervisor – I was 21 years old and I knew the director Robert Parrish from *Casino Royale* on which we both more than served our time. Central character Duffy (played by James Coburn) is an aristocrat amongst criminals who is hired by James Fox's character, a young playboy named Stephane, to hijack a boat carrying several million dollars of his father's (James Mason's) fortune.

Well, my main task on the movie was to blow up and sink this 50ft-long boat.

That's easier said than done because it was positioned in the middle of the ocean and was to be filmed from a helicopter above showing nothing else around it as it went bang.

I figured the only way it could work was by radio control, which in the mid 1960s was still fairly crude technology to be honest. We built a transmitter and receiver unit with built-in safety mechanisms: pulling the first switch would send a signal down to the receiver on the boat and trip a relay; I had to wait ten seconds before pulling a second switch which tripped another relay; followed by a twenty-second delay before a third switch could be pulled which gave a thirty-second countdown; making the fourth switch active – the detonator. I tested it out so many times and from beginning to end, the four switches took around a minute to activate and detonate.

You must remember I was going to be up in the helicopter with the cameraman so had my assistant Rex – and there were just the two of us out there – rig the boat with hundreds of gallons of fuel, dynamite, dynamite necklaces to blow the hull in half. It was a real fishing boat; the hull was made from 2in-thick timbers and 9in ribs with a big old diesel engine in it. We took it out to sea in the right direction, lashed the tiller down and Rex's job was to then connect the batteries, run to the back of the boat and get into a speedboat that was following, but just before jumping he had to flick a switch at the back of the boat. 'Keep your head down,' was my instruction, 'and pull it to make everything live.'

The helicopter then flew out and took its position with Egil Woxholt as cameraman, with me sitting at the back with a transmitter aerial hanging out the door. We started the detonation countdown by flicking the first switch only to hear the words we all dread in film-making, 'Just a minute, the sun has gone in.'

The crucial thing was they wanted the boat to sink quickly, so as soon as the sun reappeared we had to be ready to start again. Moments later, word came up and the countdown and switching commenced … and what a great explosion it was; I needn't tell you how relieved I was, and the boat went down in twenty seconds.

I felt it was a real feather in my cap, but more importantly I was so pleased to show my dad that his faith in me had been well placed. Through that film I also formed a wonderful relationship with Michael Turk, who ran the boat business, and let's just say we used to go out and have a lot of fun at night. Consequently Mike ended up being my best man twice and one of my best friends. He sadly passed away in 2016.

In my career I've been involved in a few films during their preparation period, but not during production, for varying reasons. One such movie was *Play Dirty* (1969) which was a war film set to star Michael Caine and Nigel Davenport, directed by the renowned Rene Clemént, but he dropped out and André De Toth (who though sounding French was Hungarian) came in. De Toth was a mate of David Lean, had been on *Lawrence* as a second unit director and had also been married to Veronica Lake, so had many tales to tell. We went out on a recce and probably walked over half of Israel and drove over the rest – it was just after the Six-Day War and as we ventured into all the captured territories we went over to a derailed Arab-Egyptian train that had been travelling up through Gaza, an ammunition train, which the Israelis had bombed and there was unexploded ammunition everywhere. I picked up a boot, thinking it was a strange thing to find amongst all the shells, little realising there was still a foot in it.

Between Gaza and El Arish, we were stopped by the Israeli Army who offered us a military escort because, they explained, the Arabs were shooting up cars on the road at night. I remember three of us sitting in the car humming away, terrified we were going to be shot at.

Our stay ended after Phil Hobbs Snr, the great caterer, went to Tel Aviv to look for supplies when a plane flew directly over our heads and all the anti-aircraft guns started up. Phil looked at me, I looked at him and he said, 'Airport?'

'Yeah, why not?' I replied.

Off we drove, changed our tickets and then called André to say, 'We've done everything we can, we're off now. Bye.'

The picture was never made in Israel – it just couldn't have been – and switched to Almeria instead.

As a footnote, André always wore a black eyepatch after a childhood accident cost him the sight in his left eye. On another recce to Israel some years later, just after the Yom Kippur War, he was mistaken for Moshe Dayan and kidnapped, pistol-whipped and interrogated by a group of youths. He only escaped after a physical examination established the fact that, far from being an Israeli, he was not even Jewish.

The Lost Continent (1968) was one of Hammer's less successful films, and least regarded, yet one of their most expensive and ambitious. It all started out with Leslie Norman as director, a lovely and funny man, and Dad working with an American effects man named Robert Mattey, whose main claim to fame was that he created the octopus in *20,000 Leagues Under The Sea* in 1954. It proved to be a bit of an awkward relationship – different working styles and all that.

The whole story is told in flashback, and as the captain of a tramp steamer Eric Porter wonders, 'How did we get here?' as he conducts a funeral on-board with an array of people all wearing fisherman's jumpers. Then a hurricane hits, and the crew end up adrift in a lifeboat in shark-infested seas but on finding their ship again, they are attacked by a killer octopus. It's fair to say it's a bizarre mishmash of soap opera-cum-disaster movie which is more laughable than scary, yet it got an X certificate on release.

Anyhow, Les Norman soon bailed out and the producer/writer Michael Carreras took over, and we finished the film. The best thing I can say about it was that it was a forerunner of the 1970s films John Dark made with Kevin Connor – *Warlords of Atlantis* (1978) and *The Land That Time Forgot* (1974), which were far happier and more successful ventures.

Meanwhile, *Battle of Britain* (1969) was a huge undertaking which I guess we didn't think too much about initially; it's a job and you just get on with it. Nor did we think how lucky we were to be filming with what the PR department said was the fourth-largest air force in the world, all under the command of director Guy Hamilton.

Messerschmitts and Heinkels were loaned by the Spanish Air Force, after a little negotiating with dictator General Franco. We had Spitfires and Hurricanes from all over the world, then there were our camera planes with the greatest aerial cameramen Skeets Kelly and Johnny Jordan in charge. We filmed mainly on location at North Weald Aerodrome and Duxford; I remember driving to work in the mornings and having Spitfires flying in almost touching the roof of my car as they came in to land.

Of course, filming with all these ageing aeroplanes wasn't without risk. I was at North Weald one day as a Spitfire was winding up on the apron outside its hangar when the propeller literally came off, shot up in the air and travelled across the airfield – fortunately it didn't hit anyone. On another occasion, one of our assistant directors, Vincent Winter, was up in the two-seater Spitfire, quite a few thousand feet above the ground, and the engine seized – they had to perform an emergency landing without any power. Vincent needed a change of underwear that day.

One of the air-raid sequences required the complete destruction of a hangar at Duxford and they willingly agreed that we could do it for real – but of course you only get one go at doing that. I think the feeling was the site would likely be sold off for housing development, long before plans were mooted for it to become part of the Imperial War Museum. IWe used high explosive to bring down the hangar walls and sandbags to contain the blast and debris. Naturally many planes were to be destroyed during the hangar-bombing scenes too, so after taking moulds of Spits and Hurricanes, scores of disposable wood fibreglass ones poured out of the workshops at Pinewood and were sent down to the airfield. It's amazing to think that only a small number of the planes you see on the fields were actually real – twelve Spitfires and three Hurricanes were flyers; seven Spits and two Hurris were taxiing on film; and seven Spits were used as dressing.

For one of the London Blitz scenes we used an empty warehouse alongside the Thames, near Tower Bridge; we rigged the whole thing with propane gas and magnesium flares and placed dynamite charges in the dock ... and it was very effective. Some years later on a 1980s TV series called *The Winds of War*, starring Robert

Mitchum, I was working with Martin Gutteridge and we had to recreate a similar bombed-out warehouse scene in the Docklands area and Bob Mitchum's character was to stand on the edge of the dock watching the fire rage. That was all well and good but Bob had, shall we say, a tendency to enjoy a little drink or two and realising he'd indulged somewhat before arriving on set, it called for two prop men to lie on the floor out of shot, tightly gripping Bob's ankles to ensure he didn't lean backwards and fall into the river.

One problem we didn't expect on *Battle of Britain* came when the Spanish Air Ministry wanted their/our entire Heinkel fleet to take part in a NATO exercise over the Atlantic, and then form a fly-past for all the NATO staff. It meant all the aircraft would have to revert to their original Spanish markings for two days (and back to our painted German ones afterwards). Apart from the cost, the disruption to the filming schedule would have been colossal. But producer Harry Saltzman swung into action, protesting at the highest levels, and soon after it was agreed the Heinkels would take part in the exercise, but in their Luftwaffe colours. I often wondered what the NATO chiefs thought of their fly-past.

There were several units filming at any one time: the aerial unit, a second unit which mainly involved the model shots of planes crashing and Spits blowing up in the air, and the main unit of course with all the big name stars on set back at Pinewood.

So much was done 'for real' in camera with models, foreground miniatures, and a bit of trickery but without computers – unlike the more recent *Dunkirk* (2017) directed by Christopher Nolan – and that's why today I can watch *Battle of Britain* and not find fault. It can't be bettered in my opinion.

CHAPTER 4

INTO THE 1970s

The Adventurers (1970) was directed by Lewis Gilbert and proved to be more of an adventure than I first banked on.

It was initially set up in Paris, but there was a student uprising and all sorts of unrest so we shifted to Rome for all the studio work, then moved out to Colombia in South America for around six months of location work. I'd meanwhile said 'I do' and married my first wife Jill towards the end of *Battle of Britain* so was only in my third month of married life when this film and the prospect of being a long time away from home came up, but fortunately my wife was allowed to come out and stay.

Dad and I went to Colombia to prepare, followed by the crew from Rome who flew out to join us some weeks later leaving behind Italy's beautiful countryside and green rolling hills. Arriving in Bogotá everyone then flew on to another town called Manizales where they stumbled out of a plane and into a hotel. The first location was two-and-a-half-hours' drive down a dirt track road, at the end of which we were confronted with the same beautiful countryside and green rolling hills we'd just left!

The construction manager Dick Frift had built a bridge across the river at this remote location for all the trucks and crew transport to reach the hacienda they'd planned to film in. But two weeks before shooting commenced, it rained so much that the river swelled up and washed the bridge away, meaning the only way we could get across to the hacienda now, to rig everything we needed, was on horse-back. Not only was it the first time I rode a horse, it was the first time I rode a horse across a river!

Roll forward six months, and with all the hard work under our belts in Colombia, we started winding up and readying ourselves to head home. That's when word came down from above that none of the crew's wives were allowed to fly back home on the production charter flight – they had to fly commercial. I refused to let my wife fly back on her own from such a far-flung – and fairly unsafe – part of the world, so I said she and I would take the British Airways flight from Bogotá to London. The production office arranged for the exit stamps for our passports, and off we went to Bogotá with Bob Rickard and his wife who had been told the same thing. We also met, when we arrived at the airport, Claude Renoir, the director of photography. After an overnight stay, we rose early the next morning and returned for the airport only to discover our flight had been delayed by six hours. There's only one place any self-respecting film crew member would go at a time like this: to the bar. We spent a very pleasant six hours there in fact.

When they finally called our flight, we made our way to the gate, swaying and swerving a little bit, where the immigration officer asked where our exit visas were.

'There,' I pointed to the stamp in my passport.

'That's not an exit visa,' he replied.

'Yes it is. It's a special one for the film crew,' I explained, 'as organised by General So-and-so.'

A bit of an argument developed, and whilst the immigration chap let all our wives through, he wouldn't allow Claude, Bob or myself to pass. So – silly things you do when you've had a drink – I suggested to Bob that when I said 'now' we two Brits should quietly pick up our bags and leg it out towards the plane where we could see everyone else boarding.

I waited for Mr Immigration to turn his back, grabbed our passports, picked up our bags and ran across the tarmac and up the steps.

'They're after us,' I explained to the stewardess. 'Where can we hide?'

'In the toilet down the back,' she suggested without even asking 'who' or 'why'.

Bob and I dashed through the plane and crammed ourselves into the loo, where we dared hardly breathe. Listening intently, we eventually heard a bit of a kerfuffle and then a knock on the door. A very British voice said, 'Excuse me chaps, it's the captain here. I'm afraid you're going to have to come out as they won't allow us to take off whilst you're in there.'

We sheepishly opened the door and were frogmarched off by the Colombian army. I said to my wife as I passed her, 'You're on the plane, stay here and I'll see you when I see you.'

They took us into immigration for a grilling, and of course we'd completely sobered up by then, and repeatedly apologised profusely and said how silly we were etc. They relented and said they were going to let us go, and that we should head back onto the plane where our passports would follow very shortly afterwards. We duly took our seats, breathing a huge sigh of relief, only for a chap to appear ten minutes later saying they'd changed their minds and we had to get off.

Bob, Claude (who'd watched all this going on) and I had to watch the plane, with our wives, take off and disappear into the sky.

I immediately asked if I could make a call and phoned through to our production office. I knew that the charter flight was leaving that night from Barranquilla so I told them that we would catch an internal flight back to Cartagena, and whilst I didn't know how they were going to do it, they had to wait for us and had to get us on to that charter. I was the only one with any money – typical – so had to buy tickets for Bob and Claude too, and we flew to Cartagena. I don't mind admitting we were scared stiff when asked to show our passports again, but worse was to come when I spotted the immigration guy we'd encountered walking into the departure area where he spoke to two military policemen. I think I dashed off to hide in the toilet at this point and watched through the door as the two armed MPs went over to the queue of our flight when suddenly there was a big kerfuffle and a gun went flying through the air – it was a hijacker about to board! We could easily have been hijacked as well – but thankfully we did get out of the country unscathed and, via Paris, reached home soil.

Scary times.

I should add that British Airways were brilliant and they held the plane on the runway for two hours waiting for all this to play out in the hope that we could fly with them.

Sadly, despite our best efforts and close shaves, the film was a box-office disaster. Some bright spark at the studio decided to premiere it on a brand new 747 aeroplane – and being one of the early planes it had awful headsets with a central-aisle screen, which was about 8ft wide – flying from New York to Los Angeles. All the journalists and critics were plied with alcohol at the airport and then again as they boarded – so they were fairly merry by that point – and by the time they were airborne and able to start the film the pilot realised he'd be landing before it ended, so had to circle above LA for an hour. With awful sound, a tiny screen and a bit of turbulence thrown in it's no wonder the press gave it terrible reviews which of course impacted on people paying to see it.

Whilst a lot of films I'd worked on up to this point involved months away from home, I seemed to then have a string of films come along all within a year or so which only involved me working relatively short stints – for very specific effects. The first of these was *Leo the Last* (1970), directed by John Boorman and set in a fictitious European state where Prince Leo was the last in line of a long-deposed monarchy and finds himself in London and in the middle of a counter-revolution to restore him to king.

John, who'd recently had great success directing *Point Blank* (1967), asked I go to meet him in Notting Hill where he was setting up at a big three-storey house in a cul-de-sac, and explained he wanted to blow it up and see it come crashing down.

'This explosion, John,' I asked, 'what do you want to see?'

He thought for a minute and replied, 'Something abstract,' and with that got up and walked away.

That was my brief – something abstract!

I walked around the house to check it over and discovered the walls in the basement were 2ft-thick solid brick, yet John wanted the whole place to come down, I was told, in the middle of a night shoot. I brought a demolition expert in to work with me and we drilled into the brickwork in specific places throughout the house, loaded charges inside, then sandbagged the front so there wouldn't be any blast debris coming out towards the crew. We then built a rig in the upper floor which would give the appearance of setting it alight and shoot fireworks and rockets out (that was part of the storyline). All was fine and all signed off. On the night itself, we arrived ready to make final preparations when John approached me to explain he wanted the two lead actors – Marcello Mastroianni and Billie Whitelaw – to stand in front of the house when it blew up. 'How close can I put people?' he asked earnestly. I looked around at the watching policemen, fire-brigade trucks and assembled onlookers held back behind barriers.

'How close?!' I exclaimed.

I could see John was deadly serious.

I thought carefully, did a few calculations and paced out what I felt was a safe distance, where I drew a line – the other side of the road – and told John, 'That's where you can stand the actors.'

Cameras were set up accordingly and 'Action!' was called. I pressed the button and the whole house went bang – the last brick flung by the explosion landed on the line I'd drawn. All the actors were fine and I must admit to feeling hugely relieved as although I felt sure my calculations were correct, it was still very worrying.

John was delighted and said I was the only special-effects man he'd ever met who 'has a box of matches and knows how to light them'. Although we bumped into one another in later years, and he did ask if I was available from time to time, I sadly never was.

Released in 1970, *The Private Life of Sherlock Holmes* is regarded as being one of the best takes on Conan Doyle's literary hero, directed by the great Billy Wilder. A few years ago, the film hit the headlines all over again, after the discovery of the Loch Ness monster – well, not *the* monster but one made for the film by the boys at Pinewood.

The 'monster' was the one part of the film's FX that Dad and I weren't involved with – and it was the one bit that went very wrong! Whilst we did all the little gags, as we like to call them, such as pumping in the smoke and bullet hits etc., the well-known visual-effects man Wally Veevers was tasked with overseeing the sculpting and casting of a 30ft model of Nessie, which he then took up to the loch where we were already prepping our bits. I was a pretty good diver in those days, so got into my wetsuit and slipped into the loch to help them position everything. Whilst Wally had allowed for all the elements of buoyancy in his calculations, he hadn't figured on 600ft of wet – and consequently heavy – tow rope.

When the little boat started towing Nessie from the shore and into the loch, she moved along reasonably okay, that is until the boat stopped to turn. At that moment the rope slackened and sank, slowly pulling the monster down under the water – it was like a sinking ship going down. There was a frantic scramble on board the tow boat to sever the rope before the fast-sinking Nessie pulled them under too.

That particular Nessie was lost to the depths of the loch I'm afraid and a second one was called for, with the original never to be seen again ... until recently when it was found by an underwater robot which was scanning the waters in the ongoing search for the real-life creature.

'We've found a monster, but not the one many people expected,' expert Adrian Shine told the BBC.

A second Nessie was constructed and filmed in a tank on a stage at MGM Studios in Elstree.

I was tasked with pumping smoke across the loch for the scenes, so I went out in a little rowing boat with a Bezzler smoke machine (which dated back to the Second World War), which unfortunately had a habit of blowing its lid off at any given time and consequently was attached by a chain to ensure the lid always came back – though you had to be prepared to duck down to miss it swinging at your head sometimes!

Billy Wilder was a terrific director and joyous to work with as were the cast members. Which reminds me – we later filmed at the London Coliseum for the film's ballet scenes, and I was standing in the wings ready to pump mist across the stage into the Swan Lake, watching the terrific little swans (dancers) pirouetting as they came off the stage, all terribly graceful and demure, then, as the last little one danced into the wings, she looked at me and said, very matter-of-factly, 'Oh, my fucking feet!'

I was next asked to join Lionel Jeffries's film version of *The Railway Children* (1970) which was a very sweet and delightful project shot up in Leeds; there was really only one major effect of a landslide where three trees move down a bank and onto the railway line below. I rigged the landslide by having rope ties holding everything in place at the top of the bank, and Primacord/Cordtex charges to snap and release on cue – the trees were all on hidden tracks and slid down perfectly.

With the scene in the bag, Lionel Jeffries asked if I'd stay on for the rest of the shoot to take care of all the little smoke and steam effects, but I couldn't as I'd already committed to *The Firechasers* (1971) with director Sid Hayers which, as the title suggests involved a bit of fire work. Ironically, my next film *Sunday Bloody Sunday* (1971) starring Peter Finch and Glenda Jackson, was primarily rain work – we conjured up rain all around London and being fairly low budget, there were only ever two of us, possibly three on heavy days, running all sorts of hoses from fire hydrants, with all the necessary permissions of course.

When Sean Connery agreed to come back for one last time as James Bond in 1971, he did a deal with backers United Artists to include financing two other films of his own choosing. The first (and to date only) one was to be *Something Like the Truth* which was re-titled *The Offence* (1973), directed by Sidney Lumet. Again I was involved in creating rain, but had to be pretty quick on my feet as Sidney was a very fast-working director, and often moved onto the next scene faster than anyone anticipated – meaning we had to be ready to move our rigs.

Although a critical success, *The Offence* was a commercial failure and reportedly – despite its modest £385,000 budget – didn't go into profit for nine years. Sadly, that put paid to Sean's proposed second film which he was to also direct, a version of Macbeth.

The rain continued falling for me, you'll be pleased to hear, and my hoses were next employed on *A Touch of Class* (1973), starring Glenda Jackson and George Segal. We filmed all over London, and particularly around Soho and Chinatown, where in fact I was wetting the road down one morning, trying my best to dodge the public who were walking around as the police had seemingly got a bit fed up with us asking for streets to be closed off and pedestrians halted, so didn't bother. As I was charging my hose up, traffic started coming through – talk about a helpful police force that day – and a guy in a rather nice Triumph Herald drove past, but his wrap-around bumper caught the hose and as he accelerated I found myself running as fast as I could behind him, holding the hose for dear life. However I couldn't keep up, and as we ran out of hose the hydrant was snapped off and a column of water shot 50ft into the air, right next to the camera. There were shouts and calls for me to turn the water off before the equipment was ruined but the only way I could reach the key to turn it off was by crossing through the water, the result of which saw me bob up and down like a ping-pong ball on the top.

Consequently, and perhaps not totally surprisingly, we were thrown out of Soho!

Mind you, Glenda won the Oscar for her part, so I think it was worth my suffering.

Zeppelin was a First World War film released in 1971. It involved lots of airships and we were based at MGM Studios which suddenly closed down and we moved somewhat happily to Pinewood. We also had a short scene at RAF Cardington in Bedfordshire – which has a long association with airships and balloons – with fore-ground miniature work. It also marked my first visit to Malta, where we did a lot of filming at the huge water tank, which boded me well for future adventures, not least with the *Titanic*. There was nothing very extraordinary about this movie, but the saddest thing was our American producer Owen Crump asked a buddy who was producing *The Red Baron* (a.k.a. *Von Richten and Brown*, 1971) over in Ireland if they could do a few shots of British SE5 wartime biplanes for us. It was duly arranged for cameraman Skeets Kelly who was in Wicklow filming to shoot some aerial footage, but one of the SE5's crashed into the helicopter Skeets was in and killed him. The insurance company wouldn't pay out because they reasoned they were only cover-ing the production of *The Red Baron* and not *Zeppelin*.

The Devils (1971) was Ken Russell's latest epic. He was a director who really liked to shout and scream on set – not something I was particularly used to nor liked.

He was also known for his more avant-garde ideas and as being someone who pushed the boundaries of good taste. I remember we had about thirty naked women of different shapes and sizes on the stage every day, week in and week out. One morning I walked on to the set and was quite amazed to see an electrician had his head buried in page three of *The Sun* newspaper whilst all these naked girls were sitting opposite – I suppose you become a little blasé.

Production moved up to Northumberland where there was to be a scene involv-ing a wooden wagon wheel featuring a skeleton in it, revolving. Ken said he wanted real maggots in the head of the skeleton, so I duly loaded the skull up and then slowly realised that to operate the wheel I had to be directly under the skeleton – I felt every bloody one of them falling down the back of my neck.

Ken had rather specific artistic tastes, and one of the things he hated was make-up blood, so he sent the prop guys out to a local abattoir to get real red stuff. I had to make a leg crusher to crush Oliver Reed's legs and had a set of rubber legs cast, so knowing Ken's penchant for the authentic I decided to call at the abattoir myself to pick up some real animal bones to place inside the rubber so as he could hear them snap. We did in fact have to use make-up blood, gallons of it, as there was just so much splashing around all over the set and you can't expect actors to suffer that. Kensington Gore was at that time the preferred blood of the day.

We then had the scene in the town-square courtyard where Oliver Reed is to burn at the stake, and the white-walled square is all blown up. This was built at Pinewood – it was a huge set with huge white walls as tall as my house. In the middle, I had a dummy of Oliver burning on the stake and talked Ken into putting a lot of 'black' into the explosion so it would really show up against the white walls, which he loved the idea of. I should mention the backlot at Pinewood has a very high water table and if you dig down 12in, it fills with water very quickly. So we had real problems loading our charges in the ground and decided the only safe thing to do would be to dig the holes the night before shooting, then the next morning arrive early to pump the water out and lay a plastic liner in before loading it up with gelignite, peat, black cement, cork, etc. We had lots of these holes strategically dug all around the backlot.

It was at this point Ken came over to me and explained timing was everything and therefore he would have to press the detonator himself – as in Ken's eyes there was no one as good as himself. I thought that'd be okay as I'd be holding the battery terminals and wouldn't connect them until I knew it was safe to do so. Ronnie Taylor was the camera operator and Ken told him that he had to frame on the stake with the dummy burning on it and then when cued, by Ken himself, he was to immediately, yes immediately, pan across to where the explosion would happen – remember, timing was everything on this.

All the crowd arrived, charges were placed, fires were burning and all was set. I gave Ken the thumbs up, he called action, but was so excited as he cued Ronnie to pan, he pressed the detonator at the exact same time and totally missed the shot. Well, the whole crew fell about laughing because they'd all been lectured and shouted at by Ken over the weeks about how to do their job, and here was the director himself hopping up and down screaming, 'Oh fuck, oh fuck.'

He asked if we could do it again, and of course I said yes, given time. After hosing all the walls down, pumping all the holes out and me having enough explosives in reserve to place again, we were ready to go that very afternoon.

'I'm sorry,' I said to Ken, 'but I'm going to fire this as I don't trust you.'

'Oh, all right,' he said sheepishly.

After rushes the next day Ken came to find me and said, 'Your timing was much better than mine!' For all his bluster I did like Ken very much and I respected his film-making talents enormously.

Ken was quite often his own worst enemy, and on F stage at Pinewood – a totally white set – he insisted it was to be flooded with light and insisted huge lamps were fixed onto the rail all around the top of the stage, against the director of photography's advice. They got so hot that these damn lights set off the sprinklers, but at least we had an afternoon off.

As for the finished film, I know the censors called for quite a few cuts – including masturbating nuns – before they'd give the film a certificate and allow its release but they were just a couple of scenes; there were many really quite sick ones that didn't make it into the final cut but I guess that was the reality of *The Devils*.

I did go on to work with Ken a couple more times, the second of which was *Mahler*, which we filmed mostly near Ken's home up in the Lake District. A year or two later I began *Tommy* (1975) but I didn't stay very long because unfortunately the associate producer Harry Benn was as tight as they come, and when I told him I'd need an assistant he ranted that I could surely do everything myself and he didn't have the budget for anyone else. Then there was a second request for something else and he ranted again but when I told him I needed a van to load all my gear to take to the location in Portsmouth, he told me I couldn't have one and was to put everything in the back of the prop truck. Can you imagine me putting a load of pyrotechnics and explosives in the back of a prop truck? After giving it some thought I decided I'd had enough and left the film.

I decided I should drive down to Portsmouth and explain my resignation to Ken, in case Harry decided to offer another story, and when I arrived, Elton John was filming his 'Pinball Wizard' scene. Ken tried to placate me and said I could have anything I wanted; I said, 'No, it's too late,' but asked that my assistant Nobby be allowed to continue – which he did, and he got everything he asked for!

In 1971 Sam Peckinpah brought his psychological and rather brutal thriller *Straw Dogs* to the big screen, filmed in February that year between Twickenham Studios and locations in Cornwall; the location being particularly memorable for us, shooting fifty-seven set-ups in one night – literally running from one to the other.

Sam initially asked my father to meet him for an interview, but he didn't seem to like Dad and declined to have him on the film. There was no reason given, though quite often personalities just clash and you accept it I guess, particularly as Sam had a bit of a reputation for being 'difficult'.

Anyhow, I was asked to go up for an interview – not knowing whether Sam knew I was related to Cliff – and when I arrived and started talking about what I'd done recently, I noticed Sam had this cube in his hand. It was an astrology cube of some description and oblivious to what I was saying he asked me a series of questions such as what was my date of birth, what time was I born … and he entered my answers into this cube device, which seemingly produced a result on the read-out at the bottom. The result, I guess, was favourable as Sam looked up at me and said, 'You've got the job.'

Talk about the strangest job interview ever.

There was a huge amount of shotgun hits described in the script and having just seen his previous film *The Wild Bunch,* I kind of knew what he'd be looking for, so I rigged up a whole series of test gunshots for him to approve.

'Jesus Christ,' was his response, 'where were you when I needed you on *The Wild Bunch?*'

I smiled and thought to myself I was well in with my new director and I'd like to say it was my expert planning that ensured nothing ever went wrong, but there was a fair amount of luck in the mix; a bit like Ken Russell, I knew that Sam liked to shout and scream at the crew when things didn't quite go to plan, and had the feeling he was a bit cross for not giving him the opportunity to bollock me. In fact, we lost our original cameraman after one week's filming, as he refused to be spoken to in the way Sam had.

Sam's fiery temperament and 'insane' reputation was undoubtedly linked exponentially to his intake of drugs. I'm not sure what he used as I have never used them myself. He sometimes became violent and I remember a party we had on location in Cornwall ended after Sam threw a lady across some tables when she refused to spend the night with him. At the wrap party in Twickenham I ended up walking leading lady Susan George to her car as she was in tears after Sam had said something rude to her. There were also stories throughout the film that production carpenters were being sent up to his rented apartment in London as he was continually throwing knives at the back of the doors and damaging them.

The only time I came close to a telling-off was in a scene where T.P. McKenna was to be shot at close range in the stomach by a shotgun and consequently blown backwards through the air. I built a flip rig which was a bit tricky to use but I'd done all the testing on it myself so knew exactly how it worked, brought the stuntman doubling for McKenna in early and put him on the rig every day for a week so he'd get used to it. On the night of the shoot, the stuntman was so nervous of Peckinpah that he fell off it instead of being thrown by it, and he had the audacity to blame the rig for not working properly. Realising this may give Sam the opportunity he'd been looking for to chastise me, I walked across, took my jacket off and stood on the rig – firing myself 15ft backwards and landing on gravel. 'There's nothing wrong with it!' I declared whilst dusting myself off.

That probably annoyed Sam just as much as it pleased him.

Peter Vaughan was to have his feet blown off with a shotgun in a scene, so I got an old pair of boots from the wardrobe department and went to the local butcher's shop to buy 4lb of best fillet steak. I grabbed a gallon of Kensington Gore blood and a shotgun from my workshop and drove over to Pinewood's backlot where I nailed the boots to a piece of wood and packed them with the steak and blood. I then blasted the boots from point-blank range with both barrels and took them back to Twickenham where we were filming.

'That's what really happens,' I told Sam when I showed him, 'so are you happy with that and do you want me to replicate it on set when we film the scene?'

He nodded his approval.

That's really how I got through the film – ensuring I was one step ahead of Sam and that he approved.

Our male star Dustin Hoffman was a 'method' actor, and when he had a scene where his character was out of breath I saw him – moments before the sequence was to be filmed – dashing off the stage and running up the road, in an attempt to get into character. The red (shooting) light was switched on and the order to 'turn over' given – but there was no Dustin. He'd been locked off the stage when the red light went up!

Another day he was to have a fight with fellow actor Ken Hutchison, and just ahead of the take Dustin leaned in and said, 'Hit me for real.'

'I don't want to hit you,' Ken replied.

'No, hit me. I need to react,' Dustin argued.

'If I hit you, I'll hurt you,' Ken replied.

A bit of an argument developed, and in the end Ken hit him.

So much for the 'method'. As Lord Olivier once remarked, 'Why don't you act, it is so much easier.'

It was a demanding film, that's for sure, and never had I used so much breakaway glass before, but the upshot was it gained me more publicity than any other picture had up to that point, and it led me to my first – and last – film with Michael Winner.

CHAPTER 5

EVERYONE'S (NOT) A WINNER

Scorpio (1973) had an impressive cast, led by Burt Lancaster. I was called to meet Michael Winner in his Piccadilly office, where he sat behind a desk that is probably half the size of my living room (and I've got a big living room), and there was a column in front of the desk behind which Winner had strategically placed his visitor's chair – so I was forever dodging my head left and right to see him when I was talking; it was his attempt to intimidate I think. I got up, moved the chair and carried on our conversation.

'What have you done recently?' he asked.

'*The Devils* with Ken Russell and I've just come off *Straw Dogs* ...'

'Did you stay the course of *Straw Dogs*?' he interrupted.

'Yes,' I replied.

'You've got the job then.'

He was a horrible man to work for and could be so very rude to people. He was also a control freak who, like Ken Russell, didn't believe anyone could do things as well as he could and consequently always wanted to press the detonator on any explosions. He said a few things to me that I felt were a bit off, but despite being a relative youngster I wasn't afraid to give as good back to him and with that he usually backed down.

He'd recently made a film called *Lawman* (1971) with Burt Lancaster, and stories were rife around our set about what went on. One such tale centred on Winner having his own chef on set who he upset once too often and ended up having an Ex-lax chocolate mousse served up one lunchtime. Rumour had it that he also shouted once too often at Lancaster who reportedly picked up the director by the scruff of his neck and held him over a ravine, screaming and shouting the most awful abuse back.

We were in an underground car park setting up a sequence where Burt Lancaster was going to be shot. I'd always found Lancaster to be very pleasant and personable, and when I went to his caravan beforehand to rig the bullet hits on him, I said I'd wait to connect him up to the battery/receiver as I wasn't sure what Winner was planning in terms of set-up – Winner liked to play his cards very close to his chest;

he wouldn't storyboard anything nor tell you his plans in advance – so Burt came onto the set with the two unconnected wires hanging down from the bottom of his trousers.

'Oh, I can't have this, wires hanging from Mr Lancaster's trousers,' Winner bellowed. 'That is rule one in special effects; that you don't leave wires hanging out. They should be taped up his leg.'

I looked him up and down, said 'Fuck you,' under my breath and walked off.

I strolled around the car park asking myself, 'Do I go back or not?' I decided to stay where I was for a few minutes and make him wonder where I'd gone and as I walked back in, I apologised to Burt Lancaster who said, 'It's okay, kid,' with a very knowing smile. I have to say that Lancaster to me was very professional, helpful and charming.

'If you want to show me what the set-up is,' I suggested to Winner, 'and I know which way we're going and where Burt will fall, I'll then decide what to do with the wires.'

Winner was then quite calm and talked me through it.

But then I'd hear him shouting at someone else – the wardrobe lady was in frame tweaking a costume as Winner looked through the camera viewfinder. 'You're in my shot, fuck off!' he screamed. It was so rude and so unnecessary.

We had a location shoot at Orly Airport in Paris and I drove over there to find the production department had messed up the paperwork and all of my squibs had been impounded by customs. I sat in my car for two days and then drove home, quite pleased I hadn't had to see Winner on set again.

Years later I found myself on a BAFTA nomination committee and so was Winner along with a few others. We were having a discussion about which films we thought were in the running to be nominated for special effects that year and one came up where Winner questioned who the effects supervisor was – I forget who it was, but he was obviously in the running.

'Oh, he's awful, he's awful. I don't know how he ever gets the work,' Winner moaned.

I couldn't help myself. I said, 'It's probably because he's cheap and people like you employ him.'

Silence.

Richard Attenborough was quite the opposite to Michael Winner, and a lovely director to work with, though *Young Winston* (1972) was a tough shoot. We were in Wales for part of it and those scenes called for a 'different look' (as it was a digression from the main narrative) so Gerry Turpin, the director of photography, developed a light-box gizmo that was placed in front of the lens on the camera and added a sepia hue over the film – it pre-flashed the film. It was a semi-silvered mirror placed at 45° with a light over the top shining down into the lens. In retrospect I think they'd have been much better off doing it in post-production as it caused so many problems during filming, for example in scenes where I'd set up explosions and bullet hits we had to do umpteen takes because the bloody light box kept going wrong. It wasted time and money.

In Marrakesh, Morocco, we were staying in the Holiday Inn, and there was a prop guy known lovingly as 'Mick the Bubble' (because he was Greek) and we broke into his hotel room one night and put some capsules of potassium permanganate in the shower head, so when Mick turned the shower on he was soaked by bright scarlet water. He rang the front desk screaming blue murder and demanded to see the hotel manager. By chance the manager happened to be walking past Mick's room as he threw open his door. Mick standing there, dripping wet with a bright purple towel around him, dragged the poor manager in to show him his purple bathroom. 'Look, your bloody shower, and your bloody water. It's all gone wrong somewhere ...' he was shouting.

What we didn't know at the time was the manager was actually heading to the room of one of the young ladies on the crew with whom he was having a fling, but that's another story.

The next day, laughing about it, the manager told me there was purple every-where. He poked around and disconnected the hose then undid the shower head – and showed Mick the red capsules inside. Roll forward to the next morning when Mick arrived on set, still looking rather purple, and he immediately accused me.

I said, 'Oh it wasn't me, but I'll tell you what, your boss Jack Towns who flew back to London yesterday asked me for some dye – I wonder if it was him?'

Naturally Jack got the blame and by the time I was eventually found out I was safely back home and on another film. Anyhow, it washed off – eventually.

The hotel had long corridors and occasionally on the way back from the bar we'd entertain ourselves at night with laundry-hamper racing up and down them. One night we had stills photographer Keith Hamshere in one of the big baskets and just for fun thought we'd wheel him into this lady secretary's room late at night. Keith was in the hamper with the lid shut and didn't know what was happening as we pushed him into her room, closed the door and went off giggling like schoolgirls.

Cut to the inside of the room and the secretary, unknown to us, was in bed with the hotel manager, whereupon the lid of the hamper slowly rises and two eyes appear. Keith had to extricate himself from the hamper and back out of the door into the corridor whilst apologising profusely.

The next day we told Keith that our distinguished producer Carl Foreman had heard about this secretary's room being broken into the night before, and he was gunning for Keith. Naturally young Hamshere felt absolutely awful and not realis-ing it was a wind-up, after a few hours couldn't live with himself any longer, went to Foreman's office and apologised profusely to him, whilst Carl just looked at him with an expression of total confusion.

Day of The Jackal (1973) which was a rather superb film to be involved with, cen-tred around the (fictional) assassination of French President de Gaulle.

Dad and I made the gun and the crutch that the Jackal uses in the film, over at Dad's workshop at home in Greenford. It actually worked for real as both a gun and a crutch. I ended up flying around Europe with the production showing them the different stages of assembly of the gun. I also had to teach the Jackal (played by Edward Fox) how to assemble, load and fire it.

It was just after the attacks and hijacking at Rome airport, which resulted in thirty-four people dying, that I arrived with the gun to catch a flight to Vienna. I had stripped it down into its parts, wrapped it up into a tool roll, along with screwdrivers and spanners and put it in my hand baggage. The guy at airport security stopped me and made me take everything out and I explained they were my tools – and he let me through. From Vienna I flew to Nice and from Nice I flew to London all the time carrying it in my hand luggage.

Whilst in Nice, the director Fred Zinnemann asked me to go and meet the local French effects man to make sure he knew how to handle the gun, and in the scene where the Jackal took target practice on some melons, wanted to make sure they blew up nicely.

Edward Fox was relatively unknown to cinema audiences at this time, which Zinnemann was keen to exploit as he wanted his Jackal to be able to move through a crowd anonymously, though it certainly put Edward on the map thereafter.

Juggernaut (1974) was one of the blockbuster disaster movies that were hugely popular in the 1970s. Directed by Richard Lester, it had an all-star cast including Omar Sharif, David Hemmings, Richard Harris, Anthony Hopkins and Shirley Knight to name but a few. The premise was quite simple: a blackmailer demands a huge ransom in exchange for information on how to disarm the seven bombs he'd placed aboard the transatlantic liner *Britannic*.

Bombs were needed, and happily I was called for!

I was asked to go on a scout to Hamburg to look at a ship with production designer Terry Marsh – the old TS *Hamburg* which a German cruise line had just sold to a Russian cruise company and was going to be refitted before being loaned to us for the film.

Dick Lester wasn't the original director; there was an American attached but by the time we returned from the scout he'd gone and Dick had been drafted in, which was a happy reunion as far as I was concerned. Anyhow, the daunting thing was that this was a 25,000-ton liner, 650ft long, pristine white and we were setting sail into the North Atlantic in February, looking for storms and I had to do a large explosion on the superstructure without doing ANY damage.

It proved the old adage, when the sea is calm enough to film it's too calm for the director; when the director feels it's rough enough to shoot it's too rough to film.

We had an interesting time around the Hebrides and found a few force-8-plus storms which were incredibly rough and I swear the waves were 80ft high from peak to trough, and remember being on the stern deck looking down at the sea one minute and the next minute I was looking up, being dwarfed by it.

I vividly remember getting up in the morning and going onto the promenade deck where the rail was lined with crew members, both film and ships, all looking distinctly green, then going in for breakfast and watching my fried eggs make a little bow wave in the brown cooking oil as they slid back and forth across the plate. There were only a dozen or so of us who weren't seasick mainly due to Vodka and Quells.

One morning we woke up not being able to see anything out of the portholes and soon after discovered one of the crew members had accidentally pulled the wrong lever and dumped some black heavy diesel fuel which had been blown, by the torrential wind, all down that side of the ship.

We weren't far off Stornoway so we sailed into the lee of the island and once the sea had calmed, the crew had to lower rope ladders over the side to climb down and scrub the side of the ship clean before we could carry on shooting. We did however make the headlines in the *News of the World* as the newspaper had smuggled a reporter aboard as an extra. 'High jinks on the high seas' it read and reported all the fornication that was supposedly occurring between the crew and the extras. Naturally all the film crew's wives started ringing up and consequently the guilty reporter was winkled out and given two hours to get off the ship or they'd throw him off, so we had to pull in to land.

The day came to do the explosion, with Gerry Crampton, the stuntman being thrown through the air and Omar Sharif in the foreground. I was terrified of damaging the boat and what the consequences might be but thankfully it all went off well.

We ended up in Torbay where we completed the remaining scenes. For some reason which I cannot remember, I was assigned to making sure all the cast and crew got on and off safely at the sea door, which was fine ... until one evening I was told Richard Harris was going to disembark and would I please leave the bar and go to the sea door. I waited for almost an hour and no one could tell me where he was. Eventually they discovered him propping up one of the bars. He hadn't packed so one of the assistant directors had to go with him to pack a bag in his cabin, and that's when I heard him approaching – singing Irish rebel songs. When he reached me, he gave a puzzled stare and asked, 'Why are you looking so fucking miserable?'

'I'll tell you what,' I replied quietly, 'I'm fucking cold, fucking hungry and I can't get to the bar to have a fucking drink until you shut up and get off this fucking boat.'

'Terribly sorry,' he said smiling and swiftly made his exit.

Roll forward a few decades to the first *Harry Potter* and Richard was playing Dumbledore; I reminded him – we had a good laugh and he was very sweet about it.

Surprisingly there was very little model work on the movie, as we did it pretty much all for real. When we pulled back to Pinewood from location, we built one side of the ship on a rocker in the paddock tank. I had large wind machines blowing and tip tanks dropping huge buckets of water to recreate the storm where we'd then film the lowering of the lifeboats and all the close-ups on the actors.

I'd previously been asked to work with Stanley Kubrick on *Barry Lyndon* (1975) when he was setting up the film in Ireland but was committed elsewhere so couldn't. They'd been filming for some time when I heard they were pulling out of Ireland – reportedly because Stanley had been threatened by the IRA – to Salisbury in Wiltshire. They had a 500-year-old barn that needed to be burned down so asked me if I was available. I travelled down to check out the barn and then went over to Stanley's trailer to see him – this was the first time I'd really met him. I suggested there were three ways we could do it. He immediately asked me which way I thought was the best and I told him to burn the whole barn down for real but the downside of that, over a controlled burn, was he'd need to be quick if he wanted to do a take-2 and take-3.

Stanley thought for a moment and asked, 'Exactly how long will the fire burn at its height?'

I wasn't quite sure how to answer but guessed between ten and twenty minutes.

'How long exactly before the beams start to collapse?' he asked.

What could I reply? I guessed again fourteen to fifteen minutes and it was a calculated guess because we were talking about a really old structure with solid oak beams ... fingers crossed!

Stanley nodded his approval and when the day came around, I rigged the barn and spread liberal amounts of flammable liquid all around the inside, before setting fire to it with a couple of torches. I ran and hid in a ditch whilst Stanley looked on from the camera crane.

I peeked over the top of my hide – watching Stanley as much as the barn – and I promise you, he was sitting holding his watch, I think timing to see how accurate my estimates were. Somebody up there was looking after me that day as I was within a minute of both my estimates.

It was a beautiful movie to watch and every scene looked like an oil painting.

I got to know Stanley much better some years later when his daughter Katherine married caterer Phil Hobbs, who was one of my best mates and my best man when I married my now-wife Rosie. I met Stanley fairly regularly at parties hosted by Phil and would go over to Stanley's house for dinner, which invariably ended up being a Chinese takeaway plated and served on the best silver service. Every time I ever saw him I swear he had the same green jacket on and he'd always pin me to the wall and start asking questions about other people in the film business: 'Have you worked with this construction manager?' or 'Have you worked with that production manager – what's he like, is he any good?'

He asked me to join him on a couple of films over the years but unfortunately – or maybe fortunately for the sake of my sanity – I was already contracted on other projects, though I was in LA at one point and at 7 a.m. the phone rang in my hotel – it was Stanley.

'Tell me,' he asked, 'how long would it take to put fifty bullet hits in a wall?'

'Well, Stanley,' came my considered response, 'is it a real wall or a fake wall?'

'Say it's a fake wall.'

'Is it brick or is it rendered?' I asked.

This conversation went on for about two hours and about a week later he rang me up again to ask, 'How long would it take to dress a street with piles of snow?'

'How long is the street, and are we talking a lot of snow or just a covering?' I asked.

Again, the conversation batted back and forth for a couple of hours. It was extraordinary the depth of detail Stanley liked to go into on productions – perhaps too much detail at times at the expense of the story. I mean, *2001* was a technically brilliant film but the majority of audiences who went to see it really didn't understand what it was about.

My father decided to retire from the business in 1975, as he'd been suffering from emphysema which, I believe, had been accelerated hugely when we had been on *Lord Jim* in 1965. Freddie Young, the director of photography, was quite pedantic about certain things and he liked the fog/mist effects we could create that hung in layers; the trouble was it used two chemicals, cyclohexylamine and dilute acetic acid, which when sprayed into the air would form clouds which hang together beautifully. We used the method a lot in model work because you could literally place a cloud wherever you wanted it – and what realism it lent a shot. If the stage was perfectly still without any draughts, it would stay there indefinitely. The other mist we used to use was based on hydrochloric-acid particles – titanium tetrachloride – which Freddie seemed to like more. We spent a couple of nights in Cambodia surrounded by it and as we were in the background creating it, we got the full benefit! Consequently I think Dad inhaled quite a bit; that, coupled with forty years of smoke pots and explosions took its toll and he slowed down noticeably afterwards. As the years went by, he got worse and found it more difficult. What you have to remember is we were very experimental in our approach, and nobody knew the real dangers involved. I can remember doing fire jobs on films and rolling myself up in asbestos blankets for safety – ironically you now have to obtain a special licence from the council to even dump asbestos. There wasn't a health-and-safety executive on the set back then, and we just got on with things. Dad wasn't bitter nor did he regret anything – he'd had too much fun – but it was sad for us to see him age prematurely.

Rosebud (1975) was Dad's last film and was directed by Otto Preminger – my father could do no wrong in his eyes and they got on famously well so it was a nice experience to retire after. The storyline centred on a *Newsweek* reporter who was secretly working for the CIA, using his journalistic travels as a cover story, though it was mainly filmed in Corsica and the south of France. Along with Israeli intelligence he gets involved in the efforts to release five wealthy girls kidnapped by the anti-Israel terrorist Palestinian Liberation Army from the yacht *Rosebud*. Robert Mitchum was the star.

Whilst in Corsica I remember we had a dawn call one morning for a big and fairly detailed tracking shot. The crew arrived on set at 4 a.m. to prep, and then about ninety minutes later Bob turned up – just before sunrise. He was, well to put it bluntly, as drunk as a fart.

Lots of slurring of lines went on, before Preminger walked over. He said, very calmly, 'Bob, this has to stop, we cannot go on like this.'

Mitchum replied, 'If you don't fucking like it you know what to do – fire me!'

What you must know here is this was a very personal project for Otto Preminger, because not only was he directing, he was producing and his son wrote the screenplay.

Preminger, much to his credit said, 'You know Bob, I think maybe that is the best idea. Why don't you go now?'

Mitchum left for the airport and undoubtedly expected a phone call to plead for his forgiveness all the way there and through to the departure gate, but that call never happened; instead production closed down for a week or ten days, whilst we all sat on the beach and they re-cast the role with our old mate Peter O'Toole. We re-shot the first three weeks and carried on. Preminger was one of the few people with the clout to do that and I admired him greatly for it.

Looking back on the period in which I assisted my father, I learned many things but perhaps most importantly where films and budgets are concerned, he taught me there is so very much you can do in camera. Nowadays it seems easy for film-makers to just say, 'Oh we'll do that in post-production,' and rely on computers to do what could be done so much easier, faster and less expensive and often with a LOT more reality!

Back in those days, all of our effects kit fitted into half-a-dozen flight cases and what we didn't have we made or bought locally. We were – I like to think – pretty inventive. For example, to set off a series of charges we'd have a board with a number of nails protruding – each nail connected to a charge – and would attach to the 'negative' end of a battery. We'd then take a piece of wire connected to a screwdriver, the 'positive' and run it along the nails – the quicker we ran it the faster the charges went off. A nail board was exactly what it said on the tin; we didn't have brass terminals and flashing lights.

Simplicity was often the best way, and most cost-effective. Maybe that's part of the reason I remained employed for all these years? Thanks Dad.

Around this time I was also asked to take over duties on a science-fiction film called *Phase IV* (1974), helmed by Saul Bass – the very talented graphic designer who had also designed the opening titles for a number of well-known movies including *Exodus* and *Grand Prix* – it was to be his only film as director. Shooting was set to take place at Pinewood with a location in Kenya and happily there were a few old pals on the film; Bill Cartlidge (assistant director), Keith Hamshere (stills photographer) and Terry Churcher (second assistant director) to name but three. In short, it was an offer I couldn't refuse.

My main task was to cover several acres of the Kenyan desert, in the Rift Valley, with bright yellow snow; Saul wanted it to look 'perfect with smooth geometric curves'. I conducted some tests in the UK and settled on 'Fire Foam' to which we added some very powerful yellow dye – it worked well and looked great in Pinewood. Alas, when we repeated the process in the Rift Valley, we realised there was a lot of UV light there – due to the altitude – and it destroyed the foam almost as fast as we could produce it. We then tried gluing together over 2000 square metres of yellow foam rubber and hand-brushing the surface with wire brushes; it actually worked well in the foreground. Next, we laid 60 cubic metres of sawdust to get a smooth undulating shape and covered it all with 2000 square metres of hessian which we fixed down with 14,000 6in nails, before spray-painting it all with 4,000 gallons of yellow emulsion paint. Just as we finished, a mini-monsoon hit and it rained cats and dogs for three days! Mud came up through the sawdust, the hessian shrank and the nails went rusty – it was a disaster!

With no other alternative we had to clear it all away, scrape the ground smooth and paint it yellow – another few thousand gallons of paint. Thankfully, it worked and we got everything required – what a relief!

There was one amusing incident on the film, bearing in mind everything was yellow. Lynne Frederick – more famous for her later marriage to Peter Sellers – was starring, and we were all in the same hotel, which had bathrooms with high louvered windows that opened onto the communal corridor, and one evening it was suggested (I'm not saying by whom) that we should play a little prank on one of the camera crew. We waited patiently in the corridor until we could hear him splashing about in the bath and with me on Terry Churcher's back, and Lynne steadying me from behind, I lobbed a small plastic cup of the strong yellow dye through the window. We subsequently discovered our cameraman friend was actually lying in the bath with a flannel over his face, and he didn't see the cup coming towards him, nor it landing inverted on top of his genitalia. When it did dawn on him what had happened, we could hear his shouts and yells all round the hotel – we were all hiding safely back in my room. When I returned to the UK I felt that I should ring up the cameraman's wife and explain why his scrotum was bright yellow, and that it really was a practical joke and not the after effects of a 'cure' for a nasty disease caught whilst on location – let's just say she needed some convincing.

The Little Prince (1974) was my second film with director Stanley Donen. We filmed at Elstree Studios and on location in Tunisia – quite a long way into the desert in Tozeur where *Star Wars* was later based. Again I had some old pals such as production designer John Barry, caterer Phil Hobbs and stills photographer Keith Hamshere on the film with me. Actually, Keith had an interesting moment on the stage at Elstree when leaning on a piece of scaffold talking to me and Chris Challis, the director of photography, when quite suddenly Chris and I managed to grab his arms, tied his wrists to the scaffold tube and undid his belt allowing his trousers to drop around his ankles. Chris and I then nonchalantly walked away as the stage door opened and a number of suits from the production company walked on for a set visit. Fortunately, I think that they were as amused as we were. Who said film-making is boring?

In Tozeur we didn't have much to do in the evenings except sit in the bar and play Liar Dice. I should explain: you put a dice in a large film can, place the lid on, shake and then peek inside and tell your fellow players what you want them to think you have. This particular night I was a bit late getting into the bar (very unusual), and picked up the can to give it a good shake before sitting down lifting the lid and peeking inside – only to find a live snake hissing about 2in from the end of my nose. I cleared the sofa I was sitting on backwards and it took two large brandies to calm me down. As I have always said if you dish it out, you have to be prepared to take it!

On a more serious note, I like to think we did some quite clever things on the film – most notably having the Little Prince himself walk around his little planet and watering a rose upside down. We achieved it with a very small young actor hanging on wires, whilst rotating the planet on a pole arm as the camera revolved; we had to be sure we were revolving exactly on the centre of the lens, and I stood behind the camera operating the planet and the camera revolve keeping them perfectly in sync. The mini-volcano erupting on the planet by the way was done with some dry ice, a fan, a flicker wheel and some very bright headlamp bulbs. Simplicity is everything.

The Great Gatsby (1974) was the version directed by Jack Clayton, starring Robert Redford and Mia Farrow. My main task on the movie was to set bullet hits on Redford in a swimming pool whilst he was lying on a Lilo, which was also to be hit and punctured before sinking swiftly with our star. It also called for a tasteful amount of blood (I used Kensington Gore again) changing the colour of the water. Robert Redford was very helpful and very professional, but I can remember being quite nervous because I had to be sure that each body hit was above the surface when it went off otherwise he might get a nasty bruise from the added pressure of the water on the squib. I realised that he'd had more bullet hits than most actors, after playing characters like Butch Cassidy, but great care was required. Anyhow, one day between takes I was sitting on the edge of the pool chatting to him and he told me that he would much rather be doing my job than acting; I had to agree because after my stint in front of the camera with Otto Preminger I certainly didn't want to appear on the other side of the camera ever again.

One rather extraordinary event did take place regarding this scene; I had pre-pared a show-and-tell for Jack Clayton and interested parties of a test of the bullet hits on a stunt double and the Lilo in the pool. This was a beautiful swimming-pool set built on the back of the main Pinewood house by John Box the production designer. Everyone was assembled including John and his art directors and I was waiting a little nervously for Jack to arrive. Unbeknown to me there had been a little friction between Jack and John, but what happened was still rather unusual. Jack suddenly appeared on the set casually swinging a rather large steel crowbar and before I or anyone else could say a word Jack laid into one of the set's marble columns with the steel bar (it was all plaster and lathe) and smashed it to pieces. He then tossed the bar over his shoulder, turned to John Box and said, 'That's what I think of your f***ing sets,' and walked off.

We were all left staring open-mouthed and I thought, 'What about my show-and-tell?' A few minutes later, the producer Hank Moonjean arrived and said that Jack would like to see me in his office. I rather nervously walked over and knocked on the door and Jack beaming, let me in saying, 'Terribly sorry about that old chap, just something I had to do, have a Scotch?' and with that poured me out a tumbler full which, by that time, I really needed.

We did do the show-and-tell another day and it all worked well … phew!

CHAPTER 6 (66)

THE MARK OF THE ANTICHRIST

The mid 1970s saw me getting involved with some quite big films, albeit for short stints or specific effects. One of them was *Hennessy* (1975) directed by Don Sharp and starring Rod Steiger – who was quite an intense actor of the method school and who I got to know much better in later years because he was a good friend of Stan Winston, the American make-up and creature-effects genius, and I often met Rod at Stan's dinner parties.

The female lead was Lee Remick – who was utterly lovely and was married to our first assistant director Kip Gowans – on whom I had to place various bullet hits, something she'd never had done before on a film and as such seemed terribly nervous. I placed the hits in her frock and remember watching her face, almost wincing in anticipation, as the director called action and the squibs went bang-bang-bang. On realising they never hurt one tiny bit she said, with a childlike enthusiasm, 'Oh, that was lovely. Can we do it again?'

I think I'm correct in saying that film marked the first time a production attempted exterior front-projection, and when you see it you'll see why it was the only time! It was for a scene set in the gardens of the Houses of Parliament, and involved a big explosion; understandably, the authorities wouldn't allow us to do it for real so we drafted in Charles Staffell and Bert Davey from Pinewood, who had pioneered back- and front-projection work at the studio (albeit interior). We filmed what they call 'plates' of the garden, that is to say some stock footage that could then be used in the projection process for the actors to appear in front of – a forerunner to CGI. The only trouble was the front projection was so wishy-washy that it stood out like a sore thumb; it was a good film but feels cheapened by the way it looked on screen, which was a great pity.

Meanwhile, *Rollerball* (1975) had already filmed the majority of its script at a stadium in Germany which they'd converted into the rollerball rink. The unit then relocated to Pinewood for studio work and that's when I joined the picture. There were a lot of little effects including a scene in the gardens where a gun was fired which in turn set a line of pine trees alight; we did it on what was a farm but is now the Pinewood Eastside complex – where they have built new stages – and I planted the row of trees on top of a big mound of earth, all rigged to look as though they had spontaneously combusted. A very satisfying sequence!

Then came *Lucky Lady* (1975) which was much more of a challenge; I was only 26 years old and now on a big Hollywood movie for six months! The prohibition-era comedy–drama was to be filmed in Mexico, in 125° heat, and there was already a bit of an early buzz about it in the trade press as the script had reportedly sold for $450,000 and there was talk of Steven Spielberg directing; apparently he was interested but had made a commitment to direct *Jaws* so Stanley Donen came on board. He tried to line up Paul Newman and Warren Beatty for the lead male roles but in the event Burt Reynolds and George Segal were signed. Segal then dropped out, for reasons unknown, but was quickly replaced by Gene Hackman – who was paid a huge $1.25 million fee.

Stanley was a little off-the-wall in terms of predictability, but I'd worked with him before so knew to expect that and could take it all in my stride quite happily. For instance, we were shooting in a cove where thirty boats were all rigged with fire flares, explosives, smoke bombs – you name it. I had mostly Mexican crew, with just a few English assistants, in my department and put one of the crew on each boat; I stood behind the camera with a radio ready to speak to them, because knowing Stanley, I realised we'd never know which boat he'd want where and in what direction he'd want them to move at any given moment, plus I had to be able to give the order, amongst all the chaos, to fire one, fire two etc. It was the only way to do it safely, plus as the boats were rented we couldn't damage or blow them up for real, or we'd have had to pay! We did blow up five boats we owned for the film. One of them had belonged to Harry Cohn – the boss of Columbia Pictures.

On another occasion, towards the end of the shoot, there was a big set-up – a battle of sorts – involving the *Lucky Lady* boat with all sorts of things going on; shells firing through its sails being just one. It was a night shoot and with so much activity, it took hours and hours of planning and rigging; then, just as we were about to set off from the dock, Stanley casually walked over to me and presented three new pages of script for the scene – everything we'd prepared for had gone! In a fit of pure frustration, I tore up the script, threw it onto the deck and rather petulantly jumped up and down on it. But that was Stanley and you just had to get on with it – as my old Dad said, if you don't like it then go home ...

Ricou Browning was the second unit director and wasn't averse to setting me a challenge either. He'd do it very nonchalantly and would, for example, ask, 'John, what are the chances of us having a boat tomorrow morning, with a guy in the back and an explosion blows it in half but he carries on in the rear part of the boat?'

'Okay, let me think about it,' I replied.

The next morning I'd arranged a 30ft boat and said it was rigged to blow and split in the middle, but the back part – with the outboard motor – would continue to float. I'm not sure Ricou had expected me to deliver, as he seemed – if you'll forgive the pun – blown away.

But I enjoy a challenge and working on the hoof, yet not everything quite worked out – as in the case of a night scene at sea where our director of photography, Geoffrey Unsworth, had the idea of a 'moon boat' which would – in his words – 'project moonlight across the water'.

A coastguard boat was drafted in and a tower built on its deck, at the top of which was placed a large circular mirror, set at 45° and attached to a gimbal, meaning whatever the boat did, and whatever way it turned, the mirror would remain at that same angle. He then placed a huge Brute light on the deck and pointed it up at the mirror. The whole boat was painted matte black, which meant in the dark all you could see was the circular light (in the mirror). On paper, it sounded like it could work but the fly in the ointment was the guy captaining the boat – he couldn't see where he was going because they'd painted the windows black as well!

Then, once that was sorted and it headed out to sea, there was a bit of a swell and the boat started to rock and the weights attached to the gimbal moved; I think we attempted to shoot for two or three nights but it never quite steadied itself the way it should have. It just goes to show that not every great idea works in practice.

It wasn't all plain sailing for me either, when things got fairly tricky with Burt Reynolds.

There was a scene where he was shot at by the border guards, so that meant bullet hits all across the ground where he was to be standing and running. I rigged it all up and waited for Burt to come onto the set; he arrived with an American stunt guy who I'd never met nor seen before, nor was I introduced to – I didn't have a clue who he was. Anyhow, I started explaining to Burt where the hits were and the sequence in which they'd go off; I mentioned I had a test one – just to assure him of exactly what noise it would make – right by my foot and just as I was about to tell my guy to set it off, this American stunt chap who had been standing behind Burt pushed forward and kicked a heap of stones and sand right over my squib.

'Excuse me, what are you doing?' I asked.

'I'm putting stones over, as that's what'll happen to Burt,' he answered.

Feeling a bit miffed, I told him, 'Actually, just before we shoot I'll ensure they're all cleaned off so there won't be any stones or grit that might fly up and injure anyone.'

A few more choice words were exchanged before we filmed the scene, but feeling aggravated that my professionalism should be questioned by an unknown stunt-man, I decided to go into the production office and tell them that I wasn't prepared to work on the picture any longer if friends of Burt's were going to drift onto the set and start telling me how to do my job.

Stanley Donen heard about the incident and sent for me to go down to his villa on the beach; I really wasn't sure what might ensue as he needed his stars more than he needed me, though to my pleasant surprise and relief Stanley said, 'John, you can't leave me with this lot, I need you on this film … please stay.'

We talked it through and I agreed to stay, providing the stuntman – who turned out to be Hal Needham – didn't interfere, little realising Hal had already put the poison in for me with Burt! Some weeks later we were shooting a scene at sea and I had my little FX boat with a marble gun set up to mimic bullet hits in the water. Gene and Burt were in a little boat with the camera adjacent so I positioned myself to fire my marble gun away from the actors; just ahead of turning over the cameras I was asked to row over to the camera boat. Burt started on me: 'You ain't firing no fucking marbles at me …' he shouted.

'I'm not firing any marbles at you!' I snapped back.

He was holding a bottle of Fanta Orange in his hand and threw the contents all over me, in front of the whole unit. I paused for a minute, just looking at him, wondering to myself what I ought to do. I took a deep breath, turned my boat around and went back out to sea.

Later on, I must admit to feeling really angry; I was first back to shore so decided to stand and await the unit's return and as Burt Reynolds got out of his boat and started walking up the dock, I went over to him.

'Excuse me,' I said, 'but if you think you can throw a bottle of orange over me or talk to me the way you did in front of a crew, I'll have you.'

A few more choice words were exchanged, some not very nice, which resulted in Burt saying, 'Come round the back of my caravan and I'll give you three free hits.'

I looked at him and laughed, 'You must be completely stupid. Do you think I'm going to hit you? I'd have every lawyer in Hollywood on me.'

I could see his face was getting redder and his arms started to shake in rage: 'Even when I throw orange over you, you stand there like some fucking English gentleman and make me feel that big,' (gesturing an inch between two fingers).

I knew I'd won! From that day on we never had another cross word; in fact he used to come to me at the end of scenes and tell me how good my bits were and how great it looked. He realised I was only ever trying to make him and the film look good, and ensure everyone's safety – maybe Hal Needham realised that too, in the end?

Along with some tough personalities it was also a tough film in terms of working conditions – the heat, the work on water – but it gave me a huge amount of job

satisfaction to get through the film, and also marked the first time I'd ever visited Hollywood as I had to go to LA to arrange the rental of equipment, including wind machines, to ship down to Mexico, which marked the start of my friendships with many people including Joe Lombardi and Gabe Videla at Special Effects Unlimited and Paul Wurtzel and Ray Gosnell at Fox.

The Omen (1976) was a relatively low-budget – by Hollywood standards – horror film, made for $2.4 million. My effects budget was less than £25,000 which included my salary, my crew's salary, transportation, equipment, rigs, mechanical dogs – everything. The film actually went over schedule by a month but as I was contracted to *A Bridge Too Far* (1977), I had to depart before it finally wrapped, leaving my able assistant to tie everything up. After shooting had completed, I was asked to report to Peter Beale's office – he was head of 20th Century Fox – in London, where producer Harvey Bernhard met me.

‘You were £1,000 over budget,’ Harvey stated. ‘What are you going to do about it?’

Admittedly, I wasn't impressed with his attitude, nor for giving me a dressing down in front of the head of the studio. ‘I'm awfully sorry Harvey,’ I snapped, ‘but I don't have any small change on me at the moment.’

‘Can you go back to some of your suppliers and get a discount?’ he asked, somewhat desperately.

'No! They gave us good deals to start with and I'm certainly not going back to them just because you ran a month over.'

He couldn't think of a comeback and that was the end of our conversation, though if I were to tell you when the film was released it made $90 million and no one came over from Fox to offer us a bonus, would you be surprised? But, credit where it's due, I did receive a telegram from them saying 'congratulations', as apparently every time they screened the film my credit got a big round of applause.

Harvey and I also became good friends and often used to share good wine and good food together and I was destined to work with him again on *Ladyhawke* (1985).

Budget discussions aside, it was a great film to work on, not least because it introduced me to director Richard Donner who I went on to work with – a lot – but also because there was a huge variety of effects which I am proud to say were all done for real, in camera, and that was particularly satisfying.

The chilling story centred on how the son of the devil is unwittingly adopted by the US Ambassador to Britain and his wife, played by Gregory Peck and Lee Remick respectively, when their own baby dies in childbirth.

One of the early scenes in the film involved impaling a priest – played by Patrick Troughton – who had uncovered the truth about the boy Damien's real identity. He was to meet his end courtesy of a lightning conductor falling from the roof of his church during a storm.

I built a rig outside the church in London's Bishops Park, and I have to admit one of the stakes I used to secure it to the ground disappeared into a tomb in the cemetery as I was hammering it into the ground – which gives me chills just thinking about it. The rig was positioned diagonally below the church tower with a metal bracket protruding – which fitted over Patrick's shoulder beneath his costume – from which I ran a wire up to the tower above. The lightning rod itself was made from a plastic tube over which I rolled up some paper and a sheet of contact adhesive to make an outer telescopic tube, to which I attached ferrules to help it slide down the wire. We held the rod at the top of the tower awaiting the cue to release, and then the camera followed it down until it hit Patrick's shoulder, when it telescoped in on itself – to the outside eye, it looked as though it penetrated his body. I attached a blood pump that gushed Kensington gore from the impact area, and within the rig, constructed an identical air-fired bottom section of the rod which – when triggered – emerged as though from Patrick's back, plunging into the ground below, with a bit more blood pumping out. The tricky bit was to line up the bottom rod at the same angle as the top piece of the rod and wire.

Opposite: Eddie Props, Lee Remick, Dave Tomblin, Dick Donner and Gil Taylor with Alf Joint and Dot Ford on the pads.

We rehearsed and tested so when Richard Donner called action, I timed everything to move in one clean action from the roof to the ground and, coupled with Patrick's brilliant acting, it was seamless.

All of this, I ought to add, was set in a storm with lightning hitting railings and trees in the park, before it struck and loosened the lightning rod on the roof. So along with wind machines and rain hoses, I placed a mixture of Primacord and electrical rigs with wire brushes running down the railings to give off sparks, all pulled along by a bungee rubber to give the impression of lightning travelling across the iron fence. Add in a little flash powder and few charges and I think it made it look particularly effective.

Another actor who came to a sticky end in the film was David Warner. He played photographer Keith Jennings who accidentally stumbled across the truth of the child's identity, and the script called for him to be decapitated in Jerusalem by a crane lifting a sheet of glass – the supports of which were to break allowing the glass to feather down, taking his head off as it did so. I felt it was going to be a rather tricky effect to achieve, plus the film unit in Jerusalem was minimal with the

Lining up the Priest's impaling with Dick Donner and Dave Tomblin

majority of the scenes actually being shot back at the studio in Elstree and that would mean a lot more expense. I asked if we might approach it a different way and have the glass on the back of a flatbed lorry on a building site. We could watch the driver park up, leave his cab and then moments later we could cut to the handbrake mysteriously snapping off and the truck starting to roll backwards down an incline towards David Warner, who was busy picking up the daggers tossed aside by Gregory Peck – they being the only way of killing the anti-Christ – after Peck's character refused to believe his far-fetched story.

I suggested the truck's rear wheel could run up against some bricks or stones, causing it to stop but the momentum would carry the glass backwards off it and slice David's head off.

They seemed to like my idea – and the cost saving – and asked me to press ahead.

We built a catapult rig on the back of the lorry to fire the sheet of glass – which was toughened glass because if you strike it on the edge it shatters into a thousand pieces which we thought would look more spectacular. We then adapted a shop mannequin and removed its head and adapted all the joints to make it more flexible. Stuart Freeborn, our make-up artist, made a wax head from a cast of David Warner's and I added little pockets in its neck which I could fill with blood later. We mounted the head and lined the dummy up so as the sheet of glass just caught the neck, figuring it would cause it to fly through the air. We also placed two pieces of angular steel on the construction hut behind the mannequin in order that the glass would shatter upon impact, adding to the horror.

I think I'm right in saying we shot it two or three times to get different camera angles and filmed at very high speed so that the scene is over in seconds, adding huge shock value. I'd like to think it looks pretty good on screen, thanks in no small part to Stuart Baird's amazing editing which included the head spinning through the air, 'flying into the collective nightmares of mid 1970s America' as one reviewer noted.

I employed a sculptor named Liz Moore on the film to model the skeleton which Gregory Peck uncovers in the grave of his (murdered) son, and also various dogs' heads for the same scene where he is attacked. She was a very talented sculptress and a very vivacious person and was very well known in the industry because she had already modelled the Star Child for Kubrick on *2001* and C3PO and the storm-troopers' helmets for *Star Wars*. During the course of the production, our friendship developed into a relationship and we fell head over heels in love.

Harvey, our producer, came up to me one day and said all of the religious organisations in America were praying for us as they didn't believe the devil would allow our film to be made. I scoffed, saying it was only a film and how could anyone believe all this nonsense was real? However, a number of 'strange' things happened throughout filming, and afterwards, that made me think twice but only for a short while.

Gregory Peck had a restaurant reservation in London one evening, but was late leaving the studio and couldn't make it at the last moment; it was just as well as the IRA bombed it that same evening.

Earlier, on his flight to London, in the middle of a storm over the Atlantic, Peck's plane was struck by lightning causing one of the engines to catch fire.

Richard Donner and Harvey Bernstein were flying into New York when their plane was hit by lightning and banked sideways, at which moment Harvey looked out of the window and saw a huge advertising billboard on a New York building for 555 Cigarettes and in the heat of the moment Harvey was sure it read '666'.

There was a scene in which Lee Remick had to fall (or was she pushed?) out of a hospital window and on to the roof of an ambulance and stuntman Alf Joint was going to double her. I had devised a rig which involved cutting a hole in the vehicle's roof and building a false ceiling on the inside which we covered with thick foam rubber – this would allow Alf to impact on the roof and appear to fall through to the inside. Meanwhile we positioned Lee Remick inside on a stretcher, lying with head hanging limp over the end, facing the door, covered with blood. We had also primed the back doors of the ambulance to fly open to reveal Lee. Additionally, we rigged the springs on its suspension to bounce on Alf's impact for added effect. The complete shot consisted of Alf coming out the window, the ambulance bouncing as he hit and appeared to fall through the roof and the doors flying open to reveal Lee lying dead. It worked brilliantly. Roll forward to Alf's next film, *A Bridge Too Far,* where he had to perform a roof fall – a pretty simple, straightforward sort of fall into an airbag and lots of boxes. He maintained, until his dying day, that he felt someone push him from behind – yet there was no one else on the roof – causing him to miss the airbag and land on concrete. He was in a pretty bad state and when they loaded him into an ambulance, he was lying on the stretcher with his head covered in blood, exactly like Lee Remick.

At the end of *The Omen* I left my wife – much to my parents' disgust – to be with Liz. I went on to work on *A Bridge Too Far* as previously mentioned and asked Liz to join me. We lived together throughout the summer and it was blissful.

On Thursday 12 August we went out for dinner with a group of friends, but aware we had an early call the next morning we left just before midnight. At 12.15 a.m. on Friday 13 August we were involved in a head-on car crash, with each car said to be travelling at 80mph. Everything was a blank until I woke up in hospital; my face was shattered, my nose broken, my jaw smashed – the steering wheel went through my mouth – my knee was broken, ribs and other bones too. I have hazy memories of a male nurse speaking to me and I asked about Liz, but although he didn't answer the look in his eyes told me she was dead. I was distraught.

The guy driving the other car was killed on impact – he was a barman heading home from work – and I was given four hours to live by the medics.

I subsequently discovered the accident happened on the road to Ommen. Was the film cursed? No, I really do not believe it was; there were some strange incidents, but at the end of the day you have to put it down to pure bad luck.

I was out of hospital in ten days, albeit with my jaw wired shut and my eye socket in thirty pieces, but I went straight back to work because there was nothing else I could do to deal with the overwhelming grief I was feeling. I knew the physical injuries would heal but dealing with the loss was very hard.

I had a few arguments with director Richard Attenborough about coming back to work, and he eventually agreed that I could, but insisted I shouldn't drive and arranged a chauffeur for a while, bless him. Liz was only thirty-two. She had been such a huge part of my life for such a short time, but I'll never, ever forget her.

Six weeks after the accident, one of my crew on *Bridge*, Dave Bevis, and two young effects assistants Robbie Guttridge and a guy named Alan, were in a car driving home one evening when they swerved off the road and hit a tree head-on. Robbie was killed instantly whilst Dave and Alan sustained very bad injuries. I was woken up at 1 a.m. in my hotel with the news and found myself in the same hospital I'd been in so very recently ringing Dave's parents and Robbie's brother, and doing what someone had done for me a month and a half before. That was hard. Tragic.

CHAPTER 7

YOU'LL BELIEVE
A MAN CAN FLY

A Bridge Too Far (1977) was a huge film, with a huge cast and huge requirements from my effects team of which there were twenty-five; this may sound a lot given it used to be just me and Dad on a lot of films, but there was so much going on in this movie that we actually found ourselves very stretched at times.

Set in late 1944, when the Allies seemed to have the upper hand in the war, the film follows a British and American paratrooper force who planned to take over a bridge from the Netherlands into Germany so that British ground troops could enter enemy territory, but the Allies were somewhat overconfident and it proved to be 'a bridge too far'. Anybody who was anybody was in the film: Laurence Olivier, Sean Connery, Michael Caine, Anthony Hopkins, Gene Hackman, Dirk Bogarde, Ryan O'Neal and Edward Fox ... to name but a few.

My first recce was on a freezing cold January morning to plan what would be needed – guns, ammunition, explosives (12 tonnes in total) and pyrotechnics – in fact I had our own boat travel directly from my explosives supplier, ICI, in Scotland, to Holland and unload directly. The whole unit moved out to the location in March to begin shooting in April, non-stop through until October/November.

Director Richard Attenborough was terrific with all the actors – being a former actor you could understand that – and he surrounded himself by the best assistant director in David Tomlin, the best production managers in Terry Clegg and Eric Rattray, the best production designer in Terry Marsh, and so on, to handle the vast amount of planning and production. Whilst I'd never criticise Richard, I would say I sometimes felt that I needed to battle a little to get his attention away from the actors and on to the effects, to have him watch the tests I'd lined up and get his all-important approval.

MAKING MOVIE MAGIC

One of the biggest explosions was the Amersfoort breakout barrage – you see it creeping across a huge field. We set up to film on a Dutch army range and I had something like thirty or forty explosions all lined up, each one dug into the ground and each one with 3 to 5lbs of dynamite with added peat, cork, and all manner of other things thrown in. It amounted to 100 tonnes of materials. At almost the eleventh hour the commandant of the army range withdrew permission, saying the cement dust would kill the heather! To say I was not happy would be the under-statement of the year. Luckily my interpreter told me his father worked in the Dutch government at The Hague and so I asked him to make an approach on our behalf and explain the situation. Fortunately, they overruled the commandant – who was really not happy! – at 10 p.m. the night before we were due to film.

It's a fantastic scene and I'm not exaggerating when I say day turned into night for five minutes afterwards as there was so much smoke and stuff in the air. The gratifying thing for me was that the arsey commandant was present during filming and came over saying, 'Oh that was much too much, it wouldn't have been like that at all!' but Giles Vandeleur, the man who led the tanks during the real battle was our on-set advisor and I asked, 'Excuse me sir, could you tell me how accurately that portrayed what it was actually like during the battle?'

'You've just sent shivers up my spine,' he replied, 'because I was back there.'

Incidentally the heather never suffered at all; one shower of rain and the dust all disappeared.

Following on from that scene, we then had three American fighter-bombers coming in whilst the Germans were meanwhile entrenched in the forest, with a stretch of no-man's land between them and the 30th Tanks Corp. Of course, war was raging all around with tanks on fire, explosions, tanks firing etc., and the incoming planes were to add to it all by dropping dummy bombs on the forest. I set explosions at points of impact and placed markers for the pilots to show exactly where they should aim for – my big charges. These talented guys dropped their bombs bang on target (if you'll forgive the pun) and it was one of the best sequences that I've ever witnessed. But do you know what? Not one bloody camera caught it!

Every single camera had a long lens fitted, obviously looking to capture the dummy bombs dropping, but the second-unit cameraman in charge didn't have a wide shot planned and so it was all wasted.

I was flabbergasted at rushes the next day when I realised what had happened, and pulled Richard Attenborough to one side to firstly express my frustration but also to beg and plead with him to allow us to do it again, as I felt it was just so impressive to watch. He thankfully agreed and it is in the film.

There were so many other explosions throughout – many involving rigs such as when we had to turn a jeep upside down behind Sean Connery – but perhaps the most intense were in the Nijmegen river crossing scene with Robert Redford rowing a boat which Mike Turk had built from canvas to replicate the originals only with little outboard engines hidden in the middle.

I placed one member of my crew in each of six small boats, all with a dynamite charge on a pre-determined length of string with a cork float – the idea being the float was big enough for them to see (and avoid) but the camera wouldn't pick them up. At the appropriate moment I cued my guys on the radio to let them know it was all clear and each charge sent up 150ft columns of water into the air on detonation. One went off near Redford, and Peter Macdonald – the cameraman who was in the same boat – said Redford seemed quite worried he had been drenched, but Peter just called out, 'You look fucking great, get on with it!'

We had guns firing in every direction, plus explosions on land and in the water – with barrages on the far shore – smoke machines were upriver on tugs pumping away, and there were burning car tyres everywhere to signify hits with thick black smoke bellowing out. And there was me orchestrating it all, still with my jaw wired shut from the accident speaking through clenched teeth – all very British. You may think we had days to film, but we actually had one hour between 7 a.m. and 8 a.m. when the authorities closed the river and the bridge to traffic, and they were quite strict – after 8 a.m., the traffic was to be allowed back on them both.

Because of the geography and geology of the area, whenever an explosion went off, the ground shook for miles around and for the short time of filming – and we did it twice on two consecutive Sundays – it stirred my blood. I think we had ten or twelve cameras running to capture it all, but actually had up to twenty-five cameras for some scenes.

Of course, Richard wanted some close-up shots of Redford and the other actors, so Peter Dukelow, our ingenious construction manager, built a water tank on a huge piece of concrete near Deventer. Because Richard wanted to see explosions going off near the actors, I had to think of a way to deliver impact, without harming or putting anyone in the water at risk. I got hold of some industrial steel piping, about 4ft in diameter and ½in thick, cut vertical sections to lie about 6in beneath the waterline, welded a plate on the bottom and then drilled 4in holes all around the base. I sat these on car tyres and hung the explosive charge in the middle. It had the desired effect of firing water into the air but because it was only a short way below the surface you could be really close to it and not be hurt by any shock waves. Necessity is indeed the mother of invention.

I had another accident around this time; on the bridge at Nijmegen I was sitting on railings chatting with Terry Marsh whilst awaiting a set-up change – in fact we were perched on either side of a cycle lane – and at one point Terry said, 'Sorry John, I can't hear you,' so I hopped off the rail and straight into the path of a girl on a motorcycle; its pointed front pannier pierced deep into my thigh and – according to Terry – knocked me through the air, 'the length of a cricket pitch'.

I remember lying on the ground in agony, but laughing at the sight of one of my crew running over. He looked at me and then at the girl motorcyclist who was on the floor too – and obviously decided she was better looking as he walked straight by me to help her!

Then all the unit, including Richard Attenborough and producer Joe Levine, came dashing over to offer aid and Joe's wife even proffered some tablets saying, 'You poor thing, take some of my pills,' which I graciously refused, and never really finding out what 'pills' she was on. Fortunately, an X-ray revealed I hadn't broken any bones, but I had the rest of the day off!

With Liz Moore

Looking back it was certainly one of my most challenging films and one that holds very sad memories for me, but it's a film I remain very proud of having been involved with and thanks to the sterling cast that Richard had assembled, the movie was actually in profit before we started shooting, as producer Joe Levine had pre-sold the distribution rights, country by country, and achieved top asking price everywhere. You can't say that very often in this industry.

Having completed *Bridge* I received a call from John Dark, a producer I'd happily worked with before, telling me that he was fairly advanced in preparation for *The People That Time Forgot* (1977) but was slightly concerned that the volume of effects work might overwhelm the crew he'd brought in. He asked me if I'd join the production to look after certain aspects and made me a very nice financial offer along with a wonderful location – the Canary Islands. I was tasked with all the physical effects replicating volcano lava, explosions, and so on. It was a period story set in 1919 and centred on a British expedition in the Antarctic region searching for a lost American explorer but they stumble upon a hidden prehistoric world along the way.

It was a pretty low-budget production and quite a contrast to my last one, but that's no bad thing as I've always believed technicians are often at their most inventive when money is tight. Kevin Connor – who I'd known going back to his days as an editor on films such as *Young Winston* – was directing and all these old friendships made for a very friendly and amiable working environment.

John Dark didn't hire a local caterer but instead did a deal with one of the Pinewood tea ladies who he flew over and set up with a Primus stove, oven etc., and each morning she'd go off to the market to do all the shopping for lunch. With help from the prop men, plasterers and stagehands who all happily mucked in, she conjured up firm favourites – steak-and-kidney pie, sausage and mash, fish and chips. John knew a crew with a full belly was a happy crew and that happiness often spilled over into the evenings where it wasn't unusual for us to consume a drink or two. In fact, one night I ended up in star Doug McClure's room, having consumed several glasses of something or other, along with cast members Sarah Douglas and Dana Gillespie. I remember sitting on the end of Doug's bed, glass in hand, when Dana picked up a guitar and started playing. I was feeling fairly fragile, romantically, as I was of course single again; well, the next thing I knew it was pitch black, very quiet and I realised I'd woken up in a strange bed with a body lying next to me.

I thought, 'Which one of them is it?'

I so vividly remember doing a very, very slow pan right only to be confronted by the bearded face of Doug McClure. 'Good morning darling, you were wonderful,' he said with a big grin. I was out of that bed faster than anything you've ever seen, but that didn't stop Doug spreading it around the whole crew that I'd slept with him!

One of the slight downsides to the beautiful location (sleeping mates aside) was that we were trampling around on real, live volcanoes. Several scenes called for 'fireball explosions', much like with an active volcano, so I suggested the best way to replicate these would be by digging holes in the ground – which was actually lava sand – where we could bury 50-gallon drums with a dynamite charge in the bottom, filled with petrol and paraffin. I proposed to ignite a charge on top of the drum and retreat. I must admit it created wonderful fireballs. The problem was that when you dig down into this ground you soon realise it is very, very hot so by the time you place your drum and put a dynamite charge in, the heat melts the plastic wrapping around the charge. Then when you pour petrol in, unnervingly, it starts to boil and bubble, so we used to pour the petrol very quickly, drop a charge in … and run like the clappers.

I worked with the same team again on *Warlords of Atlantis* (1978), this time filmed mainly out in Malta and Gozo, as it featured a lot more underwater work, particularly with a giant octopus! We were certainly challenged to be inventive and come up with ways of doing things on a small budget, but we always found a way and had such huge fun whilst doing so. At the end of each day back at the studio, we'd invariably finish up in Johnny Dark's office and Kevin would come in, along with Alan Hume, the lighting cameraman, and Jack Maxsted, the art director, etc. There'd maybe be six or eight of us sitting with a bottle of wine discussing the day, chatting about the next day and we probably developed things more in that hour at the end of the day than any other time. Nowadays I'm not exaggerating when I say directors sometimes don't even meet their department heads, let

alone sit and chat, and instead insist everyone deals through 'their people' rather than talk to them directly. How can you make films like that? To me it suggests a great insecurity, and that's likely why reshoots are now built into budgets and schedules, and why production companies book stage space for reshoots halfway through main photography.

Helping the Director Kevin Connor take a dip.

For *Superman* (1978) we had to make a man fly. Well, never say never.

I literally bumped into director Richard 'Dick' Donner at Shepperton Studios, where he'd just been asked to take over the movie after Guy Hamilton quit.

'What are you up to, John?' he asked. 'Because we've got to have you on this.'

Special-effects guys Colin Chilvers, Les Bowie and Roy Field had been on the film some time and so as not to step on any toes, I suggested I look after everything in America and Canada – quite a big chunk and where the first filming was to be done – whilst they took care of the studio requirements. I duly flew out on a scout to New York and Canada with Dick, John Barry (production designer) and Timothy Burrill (associate producer). We actually rented a Winnebago and drove around Canada for a week looking at locations, and because we were together all day, sitting and chatting, we developed ideas. For example, there was a gag in the script where Gene Hackman and his sidekick Otis are broken out of prison by Eve Teschmacher – she is to pull up outside the prison outer wall, in Toronto, throw a rope over, which they grab, and she drives away pulling them over as she does so. I told Dick it was a bit corny, so he asked what I'd do. 'Why don't you have them step out into the prison courtyard in the dark, and suddenly Hackman bumps into a (black) rope ladder and looks up to see a black hot air balloon with Eve in, and he climbs up?'

'Yeah?'

I continued, 'but as Otis starts to follow, every rung he steps on pulls the balloon further down – because he's so fat.'

'Write it for me then,' Dick said, before quickly adding, 'with the dialogue.'

So I sat down that evening and wrote it all out – and that's what you see in the film.

Tom Mankiewicz, the screenwriter, was fine with it incidentally and that's because he realised working together as a unit meant everyone's ideas generated so much more to the cause.

Of course, our main challenge remained how to make a man fly.

We actually flew Superman (Christopher Reeve) about 60ft in the air down 55th Street in New York City, coming down the face of a building and across to Brooklyn Heights where he rescued a cat from a tree – it was all actually achieved with harnesses and wires, cranes and rigs.

The wires were quite thin, but as Chris was a well-built and quite heavy guy we needed to be sure all the wires would be safe with his weight, so opted for slightly thicker ones meaning they had to be painted out afterwards to avoid a *Thunderbirds* effect where you see everything. We used piano wires, which I hated because despite their strength they can snap if you kink them, or don't tie them a certain way. I worked closely with director of photography Geoff Unsworth because he understood how to light things 'in or out' so brilliantly.

In another 'gag' the script called for the young Superman to run alongside a train.

I arranged for a truck with a crane arm, hung a rig from the crane with the actor playing young Superman (Jeff East) on it in an upright position – as though running – and the camera placed alongside him on the flatbed. Jeff ran at slow speed with the background whizzing by and when played back at normal speed, it looked like he was zooming by!

For another shot the young Superman had to disappear into the wheat fields with a cloud of dust behind him, as though running very fast. I acquired a track motorbike with two foot-plates on the back axle for Jeff to stand on, with a harness around his waist attached to my upper chest, so he was standing right behind me, strapped securely. I had two sandbags on the petrol tank full of fuller's-earth dust.

The camera was placed low down with the top of the wheat being just above my head. As I roared along at 60mph, Jeff moved his arms as though running, and I started tossing out sand and dust. It looked really good and all done in camera.

In another sequence, young Superman kicks a football and it sails miles away into the distance. How did we do that? Easy! I buried a big air mortar in the ground and made a wooden football; I knew if we lined the camera up carefully, the actor could run and take a fake kick (a bit like throwing a fake punch) at which point I fired the mortar and off it shot – I think about half a mile in total.

One of the other highlights for me was working with Glenn Ford, Superman's earth father. He witnessed baby Clark (a.k.a. Superman) lifting up the back of the truck. That was a crane and rig shot.

Although primarily involved in the US sequences, I became a little involved in scenes at Pinewood because in the early days of the production they hadn't quite got the flying rigs figured out and Dick would often ask me to lend a hand. On one slightly different occasion he asked for a hand when they were filming the Brando scene, with front-projection material. I'd popped across to ask Dick a question and saw Marlon was struggling to remember his dialogue, so Dick asked me to sit under the camera holding his dialogue cards (or 'idiot boards') moving them slightly from side to side so that his eyes didn't travel along the lines.

I actually worked with Brando again years later on *Christopher Columbus: The Discovery* (1992), which John Glen directed. It was the same producers behind it and rumour had it that Brando only agreed to star in it as an attempt to get the money he was still owed from *Superman*.

Back in 1978 I think we were fairly advanced, technically, and pushing the envelope particularly with blue-screen capabilities, where actors could appear in front of previously filmed rear (or front) projection. Until CGI came along, it was the most sophisticated in-camera form of optical effects we had along with front projection.

I have one other notable memory from filming in Calgary, or rather from when I left the unit there to head across to New York. I was booked on a flight to Toronto and then had to change to one for New York. As (my) luck would have it, the first plane was delayed five or six hours, for various reasons, and as we finally took off the pilot said, 'Welcome onboard our flight to Winnipeg.'

Winnipeg?

I called the stewardess over and showed her my ticket. She worked out that they'd written the wrong route down as I was in fact going via Winnipeg, so not to worry. Not to worry? Well, when the Winnipeg to NY flight was delayed, I sat in the terminal for a few hopeless hours until we were told we could board. Once on board a thunderstorm hit and despite trying several times to take off there was so much water hitting the plane that the pilot couldn't see so had to keep aborting, until he finally said we were going back to the terminal to wait for the storm to pass. Meanwhile we couldn't disembark as a direct lighting strike had knocked all the lighting off in the terminal.

Hours later we took off but when we'd reached about thirty minutes from JFK Airport, the pilot made an announcement and said, 'Sorry, ladies and gentlemen but the lightning has knocked out the power station and all the lights are out at JFK so we're diverting to LaGuardia.'

Ten minutes later, he popped up again. 'Awfully sorry, ladies and gentlemen, LaGuardia now knocked out, we're going to Newark.'

Five minutes after that he made yet another announcement and said, 'Sorry folks you won't believe this but Newark has gone down too so we're going to Toronto.'

It was the night from hell, but also the night of a famous power cut in New York where everything went down; 13–14 July 1977 was dubbed 'The New York Blackout'.

The film unit were actually shooting at the top of a building in Wall Street, on the thirtieth floor; they could obviously see the city getting darker and darker as the lights went off, and there was talk of looting and criminal activity on the news. They had generators but couldn't really shoot safely, so they called a wrap – and the poor crew had to walk thirty flights downstairs. One of the guys returned to our hotel, the Mayflower, got his key from the front desk and walked all the way up to the twelfth floor before realising they'd given him the wrong door key.

I meanwhile spent a comfortable night in Toronto and flew into NY at six o'clock the next morning when everything was starting to switch on again.

Just ahead of leaving Calgary, it was announced that Richard Lester was going to be joining the production as a producer. The reason was rumoured to be that the producers, the Salkinds, owed him money from *The Three Musketeers* and this was a way of putting him on the payroll to recoup.

Maurice Gillette, Jeannie Stone, JR, Vic Armstrong, a Wardrobe lady and Brian Warner

But of course, we read between the lines and knew we were overshooting material, and that was clearly because the producers were trying to incorporate as much for a second movie as they could, and they'd done a deal with Dick Lester to helm it. So I – along with several other crew members – went to see Richard Donner and told him that he brought us on to film and we wanted him to know that should he leave, willingly or otherwise, then we would too. It must have been very unsettling for him to have another director looking over his shoulder. However, Dick Donner stayed on throughout the shoot even though money was obviously becoming tight as, about midway through, they ditched ideas for filming scenes for the sequel and concentrated on just one film, which was the one Richard Donner edited.

The Salkinds could be a little tricky like that.

The first *Superman* was definitely the best, entirely due to Dick Donner, the second sagged a bit and then when they reached number three, they really were struggling. They so sold out.

CHAPTER 8

MISSED OPPORTUNITIES, AND ENTER 007

After *Superman* wrapped I started discussions about a project that was to be titled *Alien* (1979) for 20th Century Fox – a science-fiction horror film that was to set a standard for the genre in years to come. I'd held meetings with all the executives in London's Soho and we talked about all the big effects including the dramatic 'chest burster' scene, how best to film it and to control the creature itself. After a while the original director left and that's when Ridley Scott emerged. It was all a bit up in the air, with no start date or cast attached, though that's not unusual for big studios who spend months (or even years) developing a project only for it to fold, but I was a little wary about what might happen and when I received a call from Colin Brewer asking me if I'd like to do *Escape To Athena* (1979), I thought it was just the reason I needed to go into Fox to try and get some answers. I explained I had a firm offer on the table, and was a bit taken aback when Peter Beale at Fox suggested he'd guarantee me two films over two years and a contract – he of course couldn't say what or when, as he simply didn't know. I was more concerned what might happen if *Alien* didn't get the green light and I could end up on something I really didn't like.

Meanwhile Colin offered to double my pay. What could I say? I had bills and a mortgage to pay so I accepted.

I later discovered I'd turned down *Alien* and *The Empire Strikes Back* (1980). Not many people can say that – but at least we had a nice location in Greece!

George P. Cosmatos directed *Athena* and was probably the most paranoid director I'd ever worked with – a total chain-smoker and chain-drinker too. In the early days of the production we were in the office at EMI Elstree and when the producers asked me a question in front of George about how to do something or other, I answered it in all innocence. About ten minutes later George came into my office and beckoned me out, upstairs into his office. He then bollocked me, shouting how dare I speak to the producers without discussing it with him first.

'Hold on, George. They're the people who are paying me,' I told him, 'and though my allegiance is to you as my director, you need to trust me that I'm not going to say or do anything that will drop you in it. Everything I do is to give you the best of what you want. If you don't trust me, I'll leave now.'

From that moment he became a great friend and we got along brilliantly.

I knew the film was never going to win any Oscars, but to work with David Niven, Roger Moore, Telly Savalas, Claudia Cardinale, Sonny Bono, Richard Roundtree, Stefanie Powers, Elliot Gould and Bill Holden was compensation enough. We all stayed in the same hotel so socialised quite regularly. One morning I bumped into Niven in the shop. 'Morning dear boy,' he chirped. 'I see the beard's coming on well. How long have you been growing it now?'

'About ten years, David,' I replied. (I have always kept it very short).

He walked away giggling.

We did just about everything on that movie from blowing up oil dumps, to setting fires all over the place, launching a V2 rocket, sending motorbikes flying into the air etc. and also, between the five of us in my department, built large-scale models including a floating oil rig and blew up a model of the monastery. We built it in a little cove, reasoning it was protected from the worst of the weather and any rough seas. Well, wouldn't you know it, one night ahead of shooting, a big storm hit so I called the boys to say we'd better go out and check on things, as the model was only anchored in place. To say it was rough out to sea would be an understatement! The set was actually starting to move and so two of us donned wetsuits and swam out to tie up a couple of corners. I've been seasick on a boat but never whilst swimming before. Job done, we retired to the bar and had a few large drinks.

I was right in my estimation about the Oscar haul for the movie – it didn't worry the voters that particular year. *Alien* and *The Empire Strikes Back* on the other hand proved impressive – not that I'm bitter. I have always said you can't do them all!

Another film on which I was involved in the preparation but not the production was *Flash Gordon* (1980). Nic Roeg was both writer and director when I joined and must have been involved in the project for a year. For four months it paid my bills, but was a troubled production, brought home to me early on when I asked Nic how he saw the spaceship in his mind, as I wanted to have some guidance as to what we might come up with. He thought for a moment and replied, 'I see it as a heaving mucus-covered placenta.'

Production designer Dante Ferretti came up with some (more realistic) interesting designs but the whole production was starting to take on a very strange and possibly expensive turn with Nic Roeg's script. I think the producer, Dino De Laurentiis, became increasingly concerned about their respective visions for the film being very different and he pulled the plug. It was later resurrected with Mike Hodges and became a much more fun-filled romp.

As I said, it paid the rent for a while, but I was really rather relieved when it wrapped up as I was able to go on to a Disney film called *The Spaceman and King Arthur* (1979). They'd actually started shooting but things weren't going too well, so they asked me to come on board and help out. It was a fun script, and the thing about taking a picture over is that everyone is pleased to see you!

I must have developed a bit of a reputation for being able to step in to help out on pictures as my phone rang and I was asked to join *Moonraker* (1979).

I'd been involved in the world of 007 before, with *Casino Royale*, but this was to be my first foray into the official Bond franchise and the beginning of a wonderful relationship with Eon Productions.

Due to the (then) Labour government raising taxes massively, both the star Roger Moore and producer Cubby Broccoli had decamped from the UK and their usual Pinewood home, across the Channel to Paris. Lewis Gilbert returned to direct and his long-time collaborator Bill Cartlidge became our associate producer. Derek Meddings, fresh from a *Superman* Oscar win, was in charge of the effects work but was so consumed with miniature and model requirements that Bill felt he needed reinforcements for the floor-effects work. Politically, I'd been here before with Derek and knew I had to tread very carefully, so I asked Bill to allow me to call Derek and explain.

Derek was very understanding, even a tad relieved, and promised he'd phone his unit in Paris to let them know I was coming in to help out, not to replace nor fire anyone. I soon after reported to the studio in the French capital to discover Derek hadn't been in touch at all, and of course I was immediately seen as the enemy.

To try and placate matters I suggested I could take over the effects work with the unit in South America and Florida – far from Paris – because I realised the requirements out there needed lots of prep time and I explained having me there doing all the groundwork would take the pressure off. Whether it was the idea of me being thousands of miles away, or the fact they welcomed another pair of hands after due consideration, I'm not sure – but they agreed.

Just before Christmas 1978, I flew with second unit director Ernest Day to the Iguazu Falls where the effects crew had recced earlier in the year – earlier in the year when there was much less water in the river going over the falls. Why do I mention that? Well, there was a scripted boat-chase scene, the climax of which was Bond's boat going over the falls but with him escaping on a hang-glider moments before.

Now, Bond's boat was 20ft long and weighed half a ton – even without an engine – and had to be positioned in the middle of the fast-moving water a hundred feet or two away from the edge of the waterfall in order we could film the climactic scene. I should add it's a 350ft drop, so there was no room for error.

I took a look around with Ernie Day and whilst realising they were by now committed to the scene, I felt I had to explain to Bill and Cubby that the chances of us pulling it off were 50:50 at best, but we were willing to try. Ernie and I then flew to the Florida Everglades to check out where we were going to film the other part of

the boat chase leading up to the big end stunt, and then back to London. I should mention it was the one and only time in my life that I flew aboard Concorde – it took three and a quarter hours from New York to London and was absolutely fabulous! The plane took off, at normal speed, did a hard bank out to sea and then after ten minutes or so the captain announced the afterburners were about to kick in and we'd feel a slight 'kick' in the back. At one point, 57,000ft up and travelling at Mach 2.1, I went to have a chat with the captain in the cockpit. 'You're travelling faster than a bullet,' he told me. I actually looked it up later, and he was right! I arrived in London before I'd left New York, timewise, with a bag full of free gifts and souvenirs.

The second unit returned to Iguazu after Christmas, with a few of my guys in tow including a young Chris Corbould – on one of his first pictures. The water levels were higher than last time and I was very concerned about how we were going to get this heavy boat where it needed to be in what were fairly choppy conditions.

I took a couple of riggers and the army with us – I forgot to mention we'd been assigned our own squad from the local base. One of my guys, Johnny Morris, and I tied ourselves off on a rock and then took turns to belay each other – walking and swimming from rock to rock. Occasionally we would disappear under the water because we could never really tell how deep it was and every so often there'd be a deep hole we would fall into.

The idea was to get into position, and then pull the boat out on the ropes we'd been attached to. Johnny and I were tethered and got a little way out but saw the army guys were really terrified and getting very tired. I told the production office I didn't want to take them out again, as we were being paid and had the choice of what we did whereas they were told what to do – and that wasn't fair in such a precarious situation. I was told not to worry about them but fortunately Bill Cartlidge and Cubby Broccoli in Paris agreed with me and we did not use them again.

I'm not kidding when I say it took almost seven hours for Johnny and I to belay ourselves out to a central rock – there were no tea breaks either – pulling the boat behind us. We got it into position but in looking downstream I could see a series of rocks running the width of the river and I thought the boat might get jammed on them. Sure enough, when the time came and cameras turned over, we let the boat go into the current, it went downriver and promptly wedged itself on a rock, right on the edge of the falls.

Feeling deflated, we all headed back to shore through the rapids, a swim across the lagoon and then a climb up through the forest which was full of spiders' webs with the biggest bloody spiders you've ever seen in your life, and I wasn't sure what I was more afraid of – the water or the big furry insects.

In the hotel bar, we discussed a way forward.

It was obvious the boat needed to be moved, not only to shoot the 'over the edge' sequence, but because we couldn't even film background plates for later use with the vessel sitting in the middle of our frame.

After a lot of discussion I heard myself explaining I had a harness in my kit and the next day we should fly out in a helicopter from which Johnny could lower me down by winch, over the boat, where I'd then kick it over the edge.

So, next morning we flew out, and they dropped me – first in the water, then in the bushes and finally on the rock next to the boat. Try as I might, I couldn't move the damn thing so we had no choice but to head back to base. I then suggested the pilot should lower me down onto the prow of the boat, where there was a railing,

which I could grab hold of and then he could pull up and away over the edge, and I'd drag the boat along and over. Have you ever heard such a ridiculous idea?! Well, that's what we decided to try next.

'The winch will only hold 300 kilos,' the pilot said worriedly.

I realised there was a cargo-lifting hook underneath the helicopter so suggested they tie me on that, and then hook me on to the winch to lower me down onto the prow. Once there I grabbed the railings and as the helicopter tried to pull up, I saw my arms were getting longer and longer. It did edge out a few inches so I was reluctant to let go, yet despite the noise of the helicopter I heard a 'ping, ping, ping, ping'. It took me a few seconds to realise it was the stitches on my harness breaking.

'How many stitches have gone?' I wondered and asked myself if I should stay with the boat or stay with the helicopter.

Anyhow a quick decision was required so I let go of the boat and swung out over the edge of the falls. Johnny couldn't winch me up because the rope to the hook and the cable to the winch had spun together and had to be untwisted before using the winch. After some time I eventually rose high enough to grab the skid with my hands and John signalled to the pilot to say I was safe, but he took it to mean he should go. Tilting over the falls and down the valley the helicopter shot off, with me hanging on for grim life underneath. Who did I think I was – Superman?

Back to the bar, and even more discussion.

The next sure-fire solution we arrived at was to burn the boat. Reason being, as the structure weakened and broke up, the current would almost certainly take it right over the edge. The question remained – how to burn it?

I suggested flying out in our trusty helicopter, dropping some cans of kerosene and petrol and having made an incendiary device from the little we had available, I'd then drop it on top and we could fly off at speed before it all went whoosh.

Was I crazy? You might think so. Thank heavens it rained like mad that night and caused a swell in the river – which achieved the desired result of and washed the boat over!

A week had gone by and we didn't have any footage so we thought it best to go to Florida and continue there. As it happened the helicopter was busy with another group that day and as it lifted off from the helipad it lost control, resulting in it being very badly damaged. Imagine if that had happened three days earlier when attempting my petrol-dump plan?

So how did we achieve it in the end? With a model back at Pinewood which Derek shot!

It was a shame that Derek and I never worked together on a full-time basis because I think we could have made a pretty formidable team.

Meanwhile, back in Florida we filmed the boat-chase sequence with lots of lovely explosions going off which proved quite challenging, as although we wanted to set the bangs as close to the boats as possible, the timing was critical. A fraction of a second out and the boat, and passengers, might be seriously injured. Mike Turk and his guys were the best boat people in the business and we ended up calling them Turk's Navy. Lewis came out with Roger Moore for a couple of days of close-ups, and seemed very happy with what we'd achieved, giving everyone a pat on the back which was lovely – he was such a nice man!

One fateful morning I got up a little groggily and whilst in the bathroom I noticed a tiny black thing move across my private parts. I had to look twice because it was so small but was able to catch it and put it in a 35mm-camera film tub.

When I got to the set I asked if we had a doctor on call. An appointment was made for me at 11 a.m. where I reported to a big American blonde nurse. 'Morning honey, what's the problem?' she asked.

'Oh I've got a bad eye, I'd like to see the doctor,' I explained.

A minute later she took me through and told him I had a bad eye upon which the doctor examined me and after a minute or so said, 'I can't see any cause for concern there.'

'Oh. Whilst I'm here,' I added, 'there's just one more thing.'

I produced the film tub and showed him the little bug that I found and asked if it was what I thought it was.

He took out a magnifying glass and examined it. 'Do you itch?' he asked.

'I do since I found it.'

'I wouldn't worry too much, but if you really itch and start coming out in red blotches then go see a doctor.'

'That's why I'm here! Isn't prevention better than cure?'

'No, don't worry,' he assured me.

I went back to set and itched as well as worried all day long. I finally went over to the production office and asked Liz Green if there was a doctor on call at the hotel.

'What's the problem?' she asked.

'Oh, I've got a bad eye.'

Sure enough, the doctor arrived at my room that evening and we went through the same routine – eye, film can, bug.

'I ain't seen one of those since Vietnam,' he explained to my horror. 'I'll give you some shampoo, put it on from your neck down, keep it on for ten minutes and shower it off. Do it for a week and you'll be fine.'

Have you ever tried standing in the shower for a whole ten minutes? I wasn't taking chances; I stood there for a whole half hour!

Roll on about three months, I was having dinner with Mike Turk when the conversation turned to practical jokes. 'Ha! Did the boys get a good one on you,' he said.

'What do you mean?'

'Oh I can't say, they'll tell you.'

'Anything to do with crabs, Mike?' I asked.

Whereupon he fell on the floor clutching his stomach and almost wetting himself with laughter. The buggers had only caught six of these tiny baby crabs on the dock where we were working, broke into my hotel room and sprinkled them into the bed.

I went through all that ordeal!

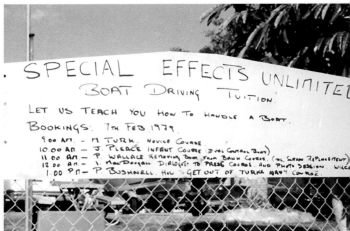

Somehow Mike, as my best man, managed to tell that story to the assembled guests at our wedding – in front of Rosie's parents! I could have killed him!

There was never a dull moment when we were around. In Palm Beach, Miami there was a rather dodgy joint called The Bloody Duck and we often went in for a drink and a little light relief, though one night it was raided by the police. We made our excuses and were allowed to go. When we got outside and were driving away we discovered that one of Mike's guys had stolen the light bar from the police car and had it in the back seat of our car ... never a dull moment ... he did return it the next day though!

Speaking of the police, we had a ranger with us throughout the boat-chase sequence and often anchored up for lunch in the Everglades. So just for a giggle, I put a row of bullet splashes alongside his boat from my marble gun. Not to be outdone, he pulled out his .45 and put a row alongside my boat. I didn't mess with him again!

CHAPTER 9

A TITANIC TASK

My next assignment following *Moonraker* was also Roger Moore's next, and our third movie together in as many years – *North Sea Hijack* (1980). It was, as the title suggests, a film about a hijack albeit of an oil rig, rather rigs. Roger played against type and as Rufus Excalibur ffolkes, showed a great love of cats, a hatred of women and an intolerance of would-be hijackers. There was a huge amount of model work including boats and oil platforms, not to mention big explosions.

Despite being set in the North Sea, we in fact filmed on the west coast of Ireland – for more beneficial tax reasons – in and around Galway.

Andrew McLaglen & Roger Moore in Galway

I set off on a recce with director Andrew V. McLaglen, assistant director Brian Cook and cameraman Tony Imi, and at the airport realised – as we were all going through security – that they were all well over 6ft tall and I looked like a dwarf standing between them. Andrew had the most enormous feet and whenever he wanted to chat, he'd stand on the other person's feet to ensure that he had their full attention – myself included. He also had a habit of leaning on my head with this elbow – I was just the right size!

We agreed that we could do a significant amount of model work for the rigs and the Norwegian supply ship that also formed part of the criminal's plan, on the paddock tank at Pinewood and I was duly dispatched to Aberdeen to take reference photos of oil rigs. When I returned to base, we set to work building the models. It was around then that producer Elliott Kastner asked me to go back up to Aberdeen with a second unit to direct some real footage, but when he saw the model footage he changed his mind because (he said) the models were so good.

Actually it was little things like the opening shot, establishing oil rig Jennifer, where I thought it would be good to zoom in on the name and then pull out to see the rig in all its glory that convinced Elliott. Plus on deck, my crew built a little rubber man and put him on a track with a little step every pace length – so as he moved along he bobbed up and down a bit giving added realism. He had a bucket in one hand and a ladder on his shoulder as I knew once they'd seen a man moving about it would give the audience a sense of scale and make them think they were looking at a real full-sized rig.

Other models included helicopters landing and taking off at night, which was achieved with the help of sound booms with the helicopter hanging underneath on wires. We used wave and wind machines to create the stormy seas and fire hoses to add a very fine spray.

I also had made a floating platform for the camera on the paddock tank so the camera moved with the water. I thought it looked great, but Andy McLaglen said, 'That shot! The camera was moving in it. The camera shouldn't be moving. It's audience POV. It should be static.'

'We want the audience to feel this is real and not a model, don't we?' I replied. 'Yeah.'

'Well, if we were shooting it for real where would your camera be?' I asked.

'On a boat, I guess.'

'And would the boat be static?'

'No, it'd be going up and down.'

It took half an hour for me to convince him it was the right thing to do; I think a lot of CGI lacks that nowadays – directors don't put themselves in a place of reality with the camera and it just looks like a video game as a result.

There was to be a huge explosion towards the end of the film – to distract the hijackers and to buy the rescue team more time – suggesting oil platform Jennifer had blown up because navy officers interfered with one of the limpet mines the hijackers had planted earlier. They were too far away from it to see the rig for real, but why would they doubt what they thought they were seeing? That was all done on the Pinewood paddock tank; we overcranked the camera to make the explosion look bigger than it actually was.

From explosions and the high seas to a more sinister film – *The Watcher in the Woods* (1980). It was certainly a rather dark tale from Disney and most memorable for being Bette Davis's last movie. Based on a bestselling book, it was a story of a teenage American girl and her little sister who become embroiled in a mystery of a missing girl in the woods surrounding their new home in the British countryside. It went through various rewrites ahead of production and became a bit of an odd, disjointed script as a result without a decent narrative. It could have been a lot more scary too, but Disney obviously worried about making it too dark in tone for younger viewers, so it fell between two stools.

One of the best shots – which never actually ended up in the film – was when the characters were driving across a wooden bridge during a storm at night and lightning struck; the bridge caught fire though the family all jumped out and ran before it collapsed, and the car dropped down into the ravine. We filmed it in the grounds of a private house in Beaconsfield – not far from Pinewood – and built the bridge for real, rigged to collapse on cue, with cameras positioned both at ground level and in the ravine below.

'Action!' came the call from director John Hough. We turned on the rain, hit the lightning and started the fire, before collapsing the bridge and watching the car fall off.

'That looked great, that looked great!' John exclaimed. 'How was it, camera one? How was it for you, camera two?'

'Just a minute,' said the cameraman in the ravine. 'I'm coming up to see you – I'm afraid we didn't get it.'

'Why not?' asked John.

'Because of the rain we left the lens cap on and nobody took it off.'

It was too costly and time-consuming to rebuild and reset, so our only option was to do it again at the studio with models, but of course being devoid of any actors it lacked all tension.

The finished film was pulled after a week on release, following terrible critical notices. Reshoots were called for and a year later it was rereleased, to not much better reviews. Sadly, it was hacked about further and various endings were reshot, but it just didn't work as a whole.

Despite her reputation for being rather fearsome, Bette Davis was completely lovely – she was by then in her early 70s and struck me as a sweet woman.

Lord Lew Grade nicked my line when I said, 'It would be cheaper to lower the Atlantic than to *Raise the Titanic*!' but I'll let him have it. The film, released in 1980, had been on the cards for some time and finally sprang to life thanks to producer Lord Grade, who had supposedly read the script by Clive Cussler a couple of years earlier when Stanley Kramer was attached to direct. Grade offered to buy the rights for his new ITC film division.

Of course there had to be a reason to want to bring the ship up from the murky depths; a plot was concocted around a rare mineral being on board which could power a sound beam that in turn could knock any missile out of the air, and in weaving a thread of Cold War tension, added pressure for the Americans to get to it before the Russians.

Alex Weldon was brought on to supervise the special effects and built various models of the ship under Kramer's guidance. Grade meanwhile said that the models were at least two or three times larger than they should be (and two or three times more expensive), prompting Kramer to quit on the grounds of producer interference. They call it creative differences nowadays. Jerry Jameson, fresh from directing *Airport '77*, was recruited in his place.

Production costs spiralled to $15 million and if I tell you the effects unit – which was stationed in Malta – had shipping container after shipping container arrive from America with more kit than I had ever seen in one place in my life, even paperclips, boxes of pencils and notepads, then you'll realise just why it was all becoming so expensive. That, plus the screenplay continued to go through rewrites – it's said that seventeen writers worked on it by the end of production – which all added to the bottom line.

At the time of filming there were conflicting views and opinions as to whether the *Titanic* had broken up as she sank, as some eyewitness testimonies of survivors suggested it did, whilst the novel assumed it went down intact – as portrayed in the earlier *Titanic* film *A Night to Remember* (1958). Five years after our film was released, the wreck of the *Titanic* was found and she had indeed broken into two pieces.

Anyhow, the script featured an opening sequence of the *Titanic* sinking and that was the first footage shot around Malta – in the nice warm summer seas, being quite a contrast from the North Atlantic in winter when the ship actually sank. The icebergs looked brown and it just felt cheap and nasty, so much so they were unable to use any of it. The unit was wound up and sent back home to America to reassemble and start again – which is when I received a phone call asking if I'd go out and look after the effects and models when the unit returned.

John DeCuir was the production designer, who used to fly in once a month and do a few sketches on the back of a serviette before flying out again. He had lots of wonderful ideas like suggesting the side of the ship should be bright silver because 'the currents will wash the sand along it and polish it'. Oh yeah?

The new models were still all pretty big – bigger than any existing water tank could accommodate – and whilst there was a rather large, but shallow, water tank at Rinella on Malta's eastern coast, it had been decided to construct a much bigger one adjacent which would blend seamlessly with the clear horizon, giving the illusion of action taking place miles out to sea. A local architect designed it – 36ft deep, 300ft across the top – taking the shape of a big oval narrowing to 90ft at the bottom. It featured a concrete ring on top and hardcore, covered in tarmac, all the way down and a concrete ring at the bottom. Though trying to seal all the edges between these different surfaces was never going to work and it leaked like a sieve with a river of water pouring out at the base.

John DeCuir had proposed to build a tower in one part of the tank with glass windows and a staircase all the way down, so you could effectively set a camera at any given level and shoot into the tank. In addition, at the bottom of the tank, he proposed a turntable that could rotate the model of the Titanic. In theory that sounded good; in practice it proved impossible – not least because we simply couldn't light 36ft below ground level. They soon ditched the idea of the tower but kept the turntable which was 6ft high and built of steel with a fibreglass seabed on top – a bit like a giant cake stand. It was built in America and shipped over, via the Panama Canal, in sections. The Malta crew then put it together and submerged it only to realise the model needed to be in position when it was dry, but the turntable had only been designed to take the weight of the model (and it weighed 10 tons) when it was fully submerged, and less heavy.

They eventually ended up having to shore up the turntable and weld it so it couldn't move – all they ended up with was a very expensive raised base of the tank which was a complete waste of time. It also made access to the underside of the seabed extremely difficult to the point that one day I was rigging some effects underneath and became trapped in there 35ft down. In the end I had to take off all my scuba gear and wriggle out backwards – quite scary.

Again, someone in his infinite wisdom had a catwalk designed to span the width of the deep tank, pivoted on one side and on a track at the other end, thereby being able to swing across the tank much like the arm of a crane. It meant you could walk across to any point and rig or hang something from above. In theory it seemed very useful. Well, almost – it was designed and constructed in California and shipped out via the Panama Canal but when they reconstructed it next to the tank they realised it was 20ft too short – because someone had changed the original architects' plans of the tank to make it that much wider, but forgot to tell the engineers who were working to old blueprints.

The production office phoned California and requested a 20ft extension but the answer came back, 'No, we have to build the whole thing again because it will change all the dynamics and won't be strong enough.'

It was dumped on the backlot and rusted away over several years.

The model of the Titanic was designed and built with internal flotation devices and at first glance it looked impressive. Though when it submerged into the tank, it sank very quickly and turned on its side at the bottom. No keel on the bottom and no allowance for the weight of one.

I redesigned it, knowing the ship had to go up and down a huge number of times over the course of the production.

In the early planning, someone had said with great wisdom, 'We'll do all the underwater stuff first, then we'll drain the tank, take the rigid turntable out, dig down another 20ft and put in a ramp so that the model can be driven up and down.'

They reckoned it was going to take months and cost a fortune – which would have undoubtedly given Lew Grade another heart attack.

I spent some time on the drawing board with a cardboard cut-out of the ship, a drawing of the tank and figured out a method of doing it using an old crane arm, eliminating the need to dig out the bottom of the tank. We bolted the crane arm to the tank floor with the model ship pivoting on the top of it. This gave us complete control over the angle and speed that it would surface but still leave it free to rock naturally. It was very effective and we filmed the raising over fifty times in all and it worked on every occasion. I placed open-vented flotation tanks in the model too, meaning as it rose out of the water all the air expanded and created turbulence which looked very authentic. The flip side of that was when submerging, the model air would compress and we would lose the buoyancy, so we had to sink it very slowly and pump air into the tanks to prevent the model sinking too fast and doing some damage. But we had complete control over how it came up and it rose in exactly the same spot every time.

Lighting underwater was pretty tricky, as already mentioned, and for the first two weeks we had almost complete black rushes until they figured it out. I also talked them into getting Arthur Wooster on board – a specialist and top-notch underwater-lighting cameraman. To keep the tank dark as it would be at that depth, we covered the top of the tank with rows of pontoons which had black tarpaulins draped between them. It worked well but you had to be very careful when you surfaced.

Next came the radio-controlled submarine models, made by Bob Wilcox, and they were great but all the testing had been carried out in fresh water and of course we were working in salt water which caused everything to break down.

We often found ourselves spending six hours a day submerged (with spare air tanks on the bottom) in the cold, and all the breakdowns only added to our time in the tank. We had a very clever British engineer who had been brought in to install a pump and filtration system to filter the salt water, the only snag being his pump drew water in from near the sewage outlet and depending on the wind and current of the day you could never guarantee what you might find floating in the 'fresh' water.

Fortunately, practical jokes helped lighten things, such as getting in early and sprinkling powdered dye into the American crew's wetsuits – after three hours below water, they emerged purple. We also found that painting the other divers' rubber mouthpieces with bitter aloes caused some funny moments as they submerged.

They in turn would swim up and undo the zip on my dry suit. Being clever, I strapped my zip down to my arm so they cut the zip off! Ricou Browning was our second unit director, whose claim to fame was he was the original *Creature from the Black Lagoon*, and he was in the tank directing a shot one day and Big John, the safety diver, swam up behind him with bolt cutters and chopped through his air hose. Ricou didn't bat an eyelid, just reached behind to switch his air bottle off, removed his harness and brought the bottle round to his front before taking the broken pipe in his mouth and switching it back on gently, and breathing direct from the hose, continued with the shot.

Although no doubt viewed as silly behaviour by many, we needed to lighten the mood because when you're working in cold water all day, every day, for six months it would drive anyone mad, I assure you and people were already getting island fever.

There was some live action filming in Greece – all the scenes on the resurfaced *Titanic* – where they'd found an old wreck and dressed it, and they asked that I supervise those scenes so it was nice to be above water for a while.

Whilst all this was going on, the casting department decided to hinge the whole film on an actor named Richard Jordan as the young dashing hero Dirk Pitt. He was totally wrong and wasn't well known enough to carry a big budget film.

Rumours of a troubled production, massive budget overspends and script rewrites, dogged the trade press so the film was pretty much doomed before it was released. The music was wonderful though.

Incidentally, the *Titanic* model was on the Malta backlot for years, and to the best of my knowledge was repainted at least fourteen times for use in other films – last time I was there, it was a Second World War hospital ship, *The Britannic*.

CHAPTER 10

THE PINK PANTHER, BOND AND ALIENS

Having not seen home for most of the year, I said that I didn't want to work on another big location movie but ended up signing on for five separate pictures that all folded one after the other including *Tai Pan* and Roman Polanski's *Pirates*. Just my luck!

A Tale of Two Cities (1980) then came along with Jim Goddard directing and Norman Rosemont producing. Aside from a great location in Paris, it was pretty unremarkable but it meant I was then available straight afterwards to join *Ladyhawke* with Richard Donner directing and *Five Days One Summer* (1982) for Fred Zinnemann, starring Sean Connery. Both were Ladd Company films for 20th Century Fox.

I obviously couldn't be in two places at the same time, so devised a plan to split my time and once *Five Days* had all been set up in the Swiss mountains, I organised for Johnny and Kenny Morris to supervise things there, whilst I headed off on a recce with Dick Donner and producer Lauren Schuler out to (then) Czechoslovakia and Bratislava and another spot high up in the Tatra Mountains. On the way up the mountains, Dick mentioned to me that he was having trouble with his neck and back and said he needed some stretching. I offered to assist.

Having checked into the hotel, I popped up to Dick's room, and the first thing he did was to ring down for a bottle of wine. I then asked him what he wanted me to do. He said he was going to lie flat on his back on the floor and could I sit behind him with my feet on his shoulders, his head between my legs, whilst I cupped my hands under his chin and gently pulled up to stretch the spine.

We were in this rather strange position when the door flew open and the waiter entered with wine and glasses. The look on his face was an absolute picture and I hate to think what he thought we were doing, but he put the tray down very quickly and literally ran from the room.

A little later that evening I received a call from Switzerland; by all accounts Fred Zinnemann said he would not shoot the planned scene of a body buried in a glacier the next day unless I was there to approve it.

'Can you be here tomorrow morning?' I was asked.

Sandy Lieberson, head of the Ladd Company, was with us on the recce and I explained that it was likely, 'Fred is just upset that I'm not there personally and he's trying to make a point.'

'I guess you'd better go,' Sandy said, not wanting his director to fall behind on the schedule.

I had possibly the worst trip ever: a fast car from the mountains to an airport somewhere, a plane into Bratislava and then a taxi through the border into Vienna, a flight to Zurich where a car then drove me to Pontresina, and then up into the mountains where I climbed the glacier straight to Mr Zinnemann.

'Hi Mr Zee,' (as he was known), 'you wanted to see me?'

'No,' he said innocently.

I respected him enormously but goodness, I had to clench my teeth.

Chis Tucker had moulded the wax head that was to be on the body that was to be discovered and I had constructed the body and given the neck mount to Chris to fit into the head when he was making it. Unfortunately it arrived in Switzerland as two separate pieces. The body in question, by the way, was of a man who had gone missing thirty years earlier and his body had now been found still buried in the ice down a crevasse. As we attached the head to the mount, a small piece of the wax at the base of its neck broke. Fortunately, the wonderful make-up man George Frost was on hand who said it was under the hairline and 'not to worry' as he'd just get a soldering iron and sort it out. Meanwhile I said to the production office, 'Don't let Mr Zee come down to see the body as we're fixing the head.'

Of course, someone immediately said to Fred, 'You can't go down there as they're fixing the head, it's broken.'

Argh!

He marched over and I could tell by his thin white lips – a telltale sign of him being in a bad mood – that he was gunning for me. 'What are you doing? You shouldn't be touching that!'

I just smiled politely and explained that the head and the body had to be attached otherwise it might turn into a horror movie.

To place our dummy, we had to climb down 60ft with it into an ice crevasse and cut a hole in the side of the glacier and dress it as though it was frozen deep inside. I looked at the ice bridge under my feet and asked the climbing guide, 'What happens if this gives way on us going down?'

'Then we all hang on by our harnesses,' he reassuringly replied.

'But how do we get out?' I asked.

'We radio for a helicopter.'

'Won't we be dead by the time it gets here?'

'Yeah,' he replied, less than reassuringly.

Let's just say we positioned the body and got out fast!

Rather spookily we then received news that the body of a man who had disappeared in the 1930s had been found in a glacier nearby. What's more, his (then) fiancée came to see the body – that was the exact same story as in our film. It's really weird when fact mirrors fiction – or is fiction mirroring fact?

Ladyhawke was postponed meanwhile because of financing issues, but more on that later.

It had been over a year since Peter Sellers had died when director Blake Edwards announced he was making a new *Pink Panther* film. Sellers had apparently been discussing another outing as Inspector Clouseau in the unproduced sequel *Romance of the Pink Panther* just before his passing and Blake obviously decided he wasn't going to let the death of his star get in the way of making a film with him.

Actually, he opted to assemble all the leftover and unused footage from previous Panther films and stitched it together with newly scripted parts for David Niven, Herbert Lom, Burt Kwouk and other series regulars – the result was *Trail of the Pink Panther* (1982).

Blake further announced he'd also shoot – back-to-back – *Curse of the Pink Panther* (1983) with American actor Ted Wass as Clouseau replacement, Clifton Sleigh.

I got on very well with Blake and always found him receptive to crew members offering ideas – particularly if they were funny ones – and many ended up in the movie; though equally he could be the most frustrating man to work for as he'd quite often prep scenes and then on the day before shooting, would change his mind totally and go off in another direction – and expect you to adapt.

One of my strangest jobs on the movie (not sure which one it ended up in) was filling a swimming pool full of jelly – it had to look like the most inviting pool, but anyone diving in would be met by a giant wobbling mass of gelatine. As luck would have it, I was having a drink at the Black Horse pub in Fulmer one evening chatting, as you do, with the landlord about how on earth I was going to tackle this scene when the guy standing next to me introduced himself as the managing director of the very company producing most of the jelly products in the UK. He proved to be a very good contact and arranged everything I needed – what are the chances of that? Mind you, getting rid of all the damn stuff after filming was another problem altogether. Jelly and ice cream anyone?

Towards the very end of the shoot I was offered another Bond film, which of course I was eager to accept, so I made arrangements to leave Blake with my key team members to wrap up the movie. Admittedly I wasn't sad to go as it had become very apparent that without Peter Sellers the franchise was dead in the water – the box office returns proved it.

Octopussy (1983) came three years after my last outing with 007 and I was placed in charge of all the effects – floor, visual and model units. I knew everyone of old, including the producers Cubby Broccoli and Michael Wilson, director John Glen, cinematographer Alan Hume, production designer Peter Lamont and so on, which made it a lovely reunion.

Fourteen of us – the above included – were first tasked with heading to India to recce potential locations where only two of us weren't dreadfully sick, and that's because I only drank neat vodka – and even brushed my teeth in it – and didn't eat any meat or fish in Udaipur. It sounds a bit drastic, but I promise you some of the crew members were still suffering many months later.

The scenes I loved working on most were back in the UK and particularly the opening minutes of the film featuring the Bede jet – a small jet plane that could literally fold up and fit in a horse box. We shot mainly at RAF Northolt, plus a bit at RAF Upper Heyford, and it was either Cubby Broccoli or Michael Wilson that had seen this tiny jet in action somewhere and thought, 'That would look good in a Bond,' as they so often did – sometimes it might be in three films' time, but a good idea was never wasted.

Not only did we have the Bede jet flying in and out of a hangar in that sequence, it was also pursued by a missile whilst being shot at from the ground. Naturally, a huge, huge explosion came at the end too.

For scenes featuring the jet entering and exiting the hangar, the pilot/owner Corkey Fornof suggested he could fly the plane for real, but on condition it was an empty hangar. He was adamant there couldn't be anyone in or around the building – but that would lack all suspense, we thought. I suggested we could build a ⅓-scale miniature jet along with a set of (foreground) miniature doors which, when positioned and lined up directly in front of the real hangar at Northolt, would allow us to fly the model in and out on wires.

Then for scenes of the jet flying inside the hangar, we bought an old 3.2-litre Jaguar car, cut the roof off, painted it a grey camouflage colour and mounted a 15ft-high steel pole arm in it, with a Bede-jet shell attached to a gimbal on top. One of my team, Johnny Morris, then laid down in the back of the car with a pneumatic control to bank the plane on the gimbal whilst I drove the car down the runway and into the hangar at 75mph. We placed a dummy in the jet's seat, though I remember Roger did sit in it once for some close-up shots – he jokingly asked if we could tell the difference. We next placed a lot of foreground dressing in front of camera boxes, machines, stuntmen running around etc. – to hide the car, and we banked it over so as the wing covered the pole when I drove in. Stuntmen started closing the far side doors, up to a 'dead stop' position which was 4in wider than the car.

'Aim for that gap, John,' was the helpful instruction.

I think it was on the fourth take, we emerged from the exit doors and onto the apron outside but couldn't slow the car down – the throttle had jammed wide open. I can remember taking a second or two to realise what was happening, but knew I shouldn't turn off the ignition as I'd lose the power steering so I ended up over-shooting the concrete apron and drove onto the grass beyond, doing pirouettes all the way – much to the amusement of all the RAF guys who were watching – until I came to a stop. When we did finally come to a stop John Morris was somewhat shaken, but not too stirred, in the back seat footwell.

Next came the big explosion I mentioned, when we had to blow the hangar sky high as the heat-seeking missile Bond had avoided by leading it in there, struck. We positioned a full-size missile on a wire at the rear of the 007 stage at Pinewood and arranged the start of a fiery explosion, then cut to a 1/10th-scale model we'd built on the backlot, filmed from a bucket suspended from a crane – swinging in a large arc – so as to give Bond's point of view as it went up in flames.

The really tricky stuff was the model flying which we'd planned to do on the back-lot where we could control external factors better. Taking off was okay as it only needed a short run, but landing was much more difficult and we had to stand with a long net so we could catch the jet as Nigel Brackley landed it in case it went into the trees beyond!

One scene puzzled everyone though. How could we film the plane being chased by a missile? This was pre-CGI, remember.

I had an idea and suggested that we build a cardboard missile, to the same scale as the model plane. We mounted a wire cradle onto the Bede jet to hold the missile for take-off and connected 20ft of nylon fishing line to a cotton reel bobbin hidden in the back of the model plane.

A short magnesium flare – to give the impression of rocket propulsion – was placed inside the missile with a simple radio-controlled trigger; I think it gave ten to fifteen seconds of burn. That meant we could get the plane into the air and Nigel would roll it over causing the missile to fall off and end up being towed by the fishing line 20ft behind. The camera operator followed the plane and missile around with a long lens and when he was ready, we triggered the flare to get the fifteen seconds of footage, if we were lucky. We did get some rather magic moments as the missile chased the plane wherever it went and for the shot of the missile over-taking the jet, from Roger's point of view, we shot a back projection plate on the paddock tank backdrop (painted as sky with a few clouds) where we ran a missile down a piece of wire – a bit like a zip-wire ride really.

We also had to construct a full-size Bede jet and fit it with a lawnmower engine to drive it and folding wings so that it could fit into the horsebox. It was used for both the exit from the horsebox and for the shot of Roger driving it into a gas station and saying his, 'Fill her up please!' line. A fun end to a really fun sequence. It all worked really well, from my point of view, and moved along quick enough for audiences not to see the joins.

Amongst the many other usual jobs – gunshots and explosions in the main – there was the train sequence, filmed at the Nene Valley railway near Peterborough, where we had to adapt a Mercedes car to run on tracks. Just after that we were doing some sparky bullet hits on the rear of the train as Roger/Bond made his escape. I was firing zirconium spark balls from an airgun around Roger who stood at the back on the train. I had loaded up my capsule gun and we were just about to go for a take when Johnny the electrician appeared – he wore glasses like the bottom of milk bottles. I asked if I could borrow them, put them on and looking like Mr Magoo, waited for the shout of, 'Turn over!' before I called out, 'Roger can you just wave your arm so I can see where you are?' I am afraid I cannot repeat his reply!

Roger used to love playing jokes on the crew, and occasionally we got our own back. In the jungle he was being chased by some baddies and a tiger was supposed to leap out and a snake crawl over his leg. I went to the prop room as I knew they had a gorilla suit there (well, what prop department wouldn't?) which I asked to borrow; I had a word with the first assistant director and hid round the back, waiting for Roger to appear. As he hid on the ground peering through the bushes I climbed on his back and tapped him on the shoulder. Roger's reaction as he looked over his shoulder was priceless and caused amusement all round.

In other tasks we also built a yo-yo saw which really worked – to a certain degree – and a second with an extending arm that could be attached to a drill to 'run' the circular part of the saw which sliced through various things. We did in fact make several yo-yos, and at the end of production we polished one of them and mounted it as a presentation piece for Cubby Broccoli, which he displayed in his office for many years.

There was a magic rope trick too, in Q's workshop when Vijay and Bond first enter and see a guy shooting up into the air holding a rope – well it was rope-moulded fibreglass on a solid-steel bar actually, hinged in the middle and – a bit like dropping through a theatre trapdoor – went straight down into the tank underneath the stage. A wire was attached to the top of the rope, to pull it up once the actor grabbed hold, and then when it was fully extended the wire was released and the actor's weight ensured the hinge opened and the desired effect was achieved.

For lovers of poison pen letters, Q invented an acid-dispensing pen and when opened, it seemingly fizzed and burned its way through anything. The acid was actually nothing stronger than tartaric (often found in wine) mixed with bicarbonate of soda to give the fizz effect.

THE PINK PANTHER, BOND AND ALIENS

As for the knife throwing, some of it was actually done for real with specialist Barrie Winship – who also gave the twins played by David and Tony Meyer a few lessons – the rest was done with wirework and I had what was essentially a catapult with a knife – the knife was threaded onto a wire and with the wire kept taut, we were guaranteed to hit our exact target each and every time.

There were lots of little challenges and gimmicks throughout; all were scripted by the way, including the guy walking across burning coals (in actuality some lights, smoke and a little flame to give the effect), a sword swallower (the sword blade was made from a steel tape measure), bed of nails (rubber ones) ... and so forth. I like to think we were inventive and certainly all our efforts were appreciated by Cubby; I still maintain he was the best producer I've ever worked with because whenever we sat around a table for a production meeting, he would invariably sit at the back and just listen to the usual chat going on when, all of a sudden, he'd pipe up with, 'That's what we'll do,' or, 'No, we won't do that' – and the decision was made. Whatever he backed us on, he backed us totally though he always had the knack of knowing what would work and he always surrounded himself with good people. He was one of the nicest people you'd ever hope to meet and he knew everybody on his set. I, along with many others, miss him.

Just as the titles on *Octopussy* promised James Bond would return, *Ladyhawke* (1985) returned into my life! It was good to be back with Dick Donner and some new technology; this was the first film I'd ever seen video playback on set. It's a great piece of technology, essentially showing on a small video screen what the film camera was seeing and though taken for granted by anyone who owns a digital camera nowadays, prior to this innovation you had two choices if you wanted to see what a set-up looked like – stand or sit next to the camera (which is what most directors did) or look through the viewfinder. Other than that, you had to wait to see the rushes the next day. Though one of the unfortunate aspects of playback is that it can make directors lazy – I'm often amazed to see them squinting at a 10in screen during the middle of a take rather than raising their head to watch it all going on in front of them – the technology has improved enormously over the intervening years and it is now a vital piece of filming equipment.

The beauty of working with Dick Donner was that whilst he used playback as a helpful tool and aid, he always relied on his judgement coupled with the continuity lady – Elaine Schreyeck in this case – and his cinematographer to name the best takes to print.

We shot in Italy over a six-month period and it was one of those lovely films where everybody got on so well, in particular the lead cast: Matthew Broderick as Philippe Gaston, Kurt Russell who was to play Captain Etienne of Navarre (but he decided to leave the movie and was replaced by Rutger Hauer), and Michelle

John Brown operating the mechanical hawk

Pfeiffer as Isabeau of Anjou. Also, how could one complain about spending all that time in Rome, Tuscany and the Dolomites – beautiful country and wonderful food.

Back in those days the effects department also used to make most of the creatures that were required for a film and on this occasion, we made several dummy hawks operated by radio control.

Dick Donner remains to this day the best director I ever worked with and I think that was because, apart from being great fun to be around, he managed to get the most out of me in terms of creativity and accordingly, I had a great feeling of job satisfaction.

We wrapped on *Ladyhawke* just before Christmas and in the new year began preparation on *A View to a Kill* (1985) which, happily, I had been asked to join the Bond team for again. It was directed by John Glen although there was talk Roger Moore might not be donning the famous tuxedo, but unbeknown to us, his agent and the producers were playing a bit of a game of 'negotiation poker'. Eventually Roger got the deal his people felt he was worth and he signed on to play 007 one more time.

We scouted all over Iceland and saw some amazing scenery, and filming started on an ice lake at the bottom of a glacier near a town called Höfn.

There were lots of model requirements on the picture, particularly involving the villain Zorin's airship, which ended up in the movie's climax on top of the Golden Gate Bridge in San Francisco. The wonderful thing about the Bonds was that there were always storyboards detailing every shot the director envisaged, and I could sit down with John Glen to discuss what the best way of achieving those shots were and how much they might cost, or how there might be another way of doing it that would look better and/or cost less.

Again, much of it was smoke and mirrors as the majority of the shots involving the actors was all filmed on the Pinewood backlot. For the models, we had three different scales of airship, one very small about 4ft long, a larger fibreglass one that was about 10ft long and a large 40ft-long one that was used along with a huge 150ft-wide panoramic photographic cut-out of the San Francisco Bay skyline as a backdrop, with a section of bridge built in the foreground with the airship hung or tethered on wires – which had to be painted out in those days. I say hung or tethered because for some shots we would fill the 40ft model with air and hang it from above and other days when we might see those wires, we would fill it with helium and tether it from below. The ship had an 18in inlet tube about 10ft long that I had to crawl through to adjust the envelope when we were filling the ship with gas; not a problem when it was air but when it was helium I had to use a diving tank and demand valve to breathe through. On one occasion I somehow breathed too much helium and almost passed out inside. For the finale when the ship blew up, we filled it full of hydrogen which helped to make the explosion even bigger.

Building a model didn't mean we got away without filming on the Golden Gate Bridge itself because I had to shoot the background plates for the process work and some live-action cuts with stunt doubles. To get to the top we had to go up in a tiny lift, then walk 100ft down along one of the cables where we built a wooden platform for the VistaVision camera. On one of the recces I took our helicopter cameraman up to see what he'd be filming. It took seven-and-a-half minutes to ascend – when you're forever hoping there isn't an earthquake – then I led him up a ladder, along a catwalk, up another ladder, out of a hatch to witness the most wonderful 360° fisheye view some 746ft above sea level. As I watched him climb out of the hatch, his face paled and he admitted he couldn't do it because he hated heights; strange when he could sit all day with his legs dangling out of a helicopter to shoot the aerial work. Consequently, I ended up with two great cameramen, one for the helicopter filming and one for the land- or bridge-based work. I should add that the giant cables holding the bridge up, bounce up and down when trucks cross, making standing on them feel quite strange especially at 5 a.m. when they are soaking wet. I also shot all the helicopter plates and my pilot was a wonderful man named Rick Holley; a veteran of the Vietnam War, he was sadly killed a short while later whilst working on another movie.

Back on terra firma, there were lots of scenes set on the streets of San Francisco, the main one being a fire-engine chase and setting City Hall on fire just above Mayor Diana Feinstein's office. We achieved it all with just a small UK crew and an American effects team led by Larry Cavanaugh who I worked with again on *Licence to Kill* (1989) and *Cliffhanger* (1993). To make it look as though the building was on fire, we clad the office windows with fireproof board and placed fire bars burning propane gas in them along with fishtail burners on the roof and**,** to get that incandescent glow that you see from big fires**,** we burnt large 6in-diameter magnesium flares that I had specially made for me. Adding additional smoke gave us a wonderful glow. I must admit we had the most wonderful help and collaboration from the authorities and as a token of his appreciation, producer Cubby Broccoli held the world premiere in the city.

Meanwhile, back at Pinewood there was lots to do and it wasn't helped when we received news that the 007 stage had burned to the ground; a fire broke out on the set of Ridley Scott's film *Legend*. Our production designer Peter Lamont had to hurriedly move things around whilst he supervised the rebuilding of the stage, on which one of our biggest sets was to be constructed – for the cavernous mine-flooding sequence. Part of it was done for real, with water flooding the tank inside the stage, and the rest with a model. One of the shots I was most pleased with was done during the main flooding, when I wanted to get some life into the model. To achieve this, I mounted a small triangular mirror into the model set which reflected two doubles of the baddies – Christopher Walken and his henchman, played by Patrick Bauchau. They were in fact standing some distance behind the camera on a rostrum in front of

a small piece of matching rock. This put their image perfectly in scale into the middle of the model set and as long as they held their machine guns left-handed because of the mirror image it looked terrific. Smoke and mirrors!

The exterior of that set was filmed at Amberley chalk pits, where we blew Grace Jones up. That explosion was full size, and after we filmed Grace coming out on the trolley, we cut, took her off and replaced her with a dummy which, on the next shot, we towed out a bit more and blew up with a large charge of high explosive. Roger Moore took a great interest in that scene for some reason.

Oh, of course there were the usual Q branch gimmicks. This time around, the height of technology allowed us to create a remote control 'Snooper' – a surveillance device in the form of a K9. Then there were sunglasses that could see through mirrored glass (just polarised), a credit-card lock pick (didn't work for real), a tiny camera built into a ring (well, that didn't work either), but they were all plausible and a lot actually made it into the script depending on what Jerry Juroe, Eon's marketing director, could get in terms of product placement. Deals were always going on. One was with *People* magazine, which was strategically placed on Zorin's desk – there was a big photo of Zorin on the front cover, and a small one of me in top corner with 'A Real-Life JR' as the caption. Thanks Jerry!

John Glen had seen someone perform a dancing-butterfly act (fake butterflies on the end of fishing rods) and thought it was a fun idea, so tracked down the Frenchman who was then running a hotel just outside Paris. We all met there to stay the night, have a dinner and to see an open-air demonstration. Sadly, by the time we finished our delicious meal and took our seats outside, it was pouring with rain – we all got soaked along with the paper butterflies. Anyhow, we invited him to Pinewood where Peter had built the Eiffel Tower restaurant set and with a bit of finessing, it all worked nicely and that's what you see in the film – which turned out to be Roger's last outing as 007.

Aliens (1986) was of course a follow-up to Alien – the film I never ended up working on, much to my regret. Aliens was directed by James Cameron who had a reputation for being a hard taskmaster. Peter Lamont and I flew out to LA early on to meet with Jim, his wife and producer, Gale Anne Hurd and Stan Winston – the special make-up effects genius – to talk about everything. This happily coincided with the premiere of A View to a Kill and Cubby flew us both up to San Francisco and a good time was had by all, as the saying goes.

Jim was the most wonderful, talented director but could be a little all-consuming as I discovered when he started getting fussy about the screw heads in the boots of the power loader – the P-5000 Powered Work Loader was a mechanised exo-skeleton used for lifting heavy materials and objects. Jim had designed it and gave

  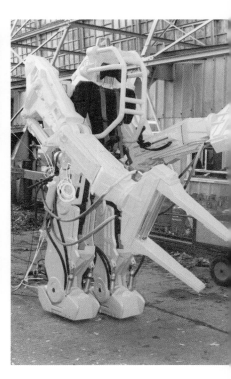

Reunion at the Albert Hall with Pete Lamont, Jim Cameron, Ludwig Wicki, Sigourney, Gale Anne Hurd and JR

a us a concept drawing to follow but the small details, such as him deciding if the screw heads should be crosshead or flat was just one example of his attention to minute detail going a little too far. In fact I went to Gale and said, 'With the greatest of respect to Jim, if he carries on like this we're not going to be ready to shoot. You've got to get him off my back.'

The following Friday, three bottles of champagne turned up at the workshop with the message, 'Building Power Loaders is thirsty work – have one on me, Love Jim.'

Jim did have a good sense of humour as it happens, and always used to involve the crew in asking them what they thought about certain set-ups. We were working on the scene at the very beginning of the film where they find Sigourney Weaver asleep and Jim went in over the weekend prior and dressed the interior of the pods – the beds in freezers if you like – with coloured glitter; it looked like Christmas. I came on the set only for Jim to ask, 'What do you think of this, John?'

'It looks a bit like Santa's grotto,' I replied with a grin.

In fact I was told off three times that day for whistling 'I'm Dreaming of a White Christmas'.

I decided to go one further and popped over to the props department to get a set of Christmas-tree lights, with which I dressed the outside window of the said spaceship. When Jim called, 'Turn over,' I switched the lights on. The crew fell about and Jim, I must admit, took it really well.

When we were trying to figure out how to make the legs easier to move and arms a bit lighter for Sigourney, we built a stuntman, John Lees, into the main body of the power-loader machine; we stood him inside what looked like the metalwork of the body and covered him up with the rubber backrest where the operator/ Sigourney stood. All the movements were rehearsed and John helped bear the weight. However, one day I worked out that Sigourney's bum was right up against John's crotch – separated only by a bit of foam rubber. Without either of them knowing, though I did tell Jim Cameron, I took a football bladder and taped it in position on the back rest with a little air hose coming down the power loader's leg. Once they were both inside, they couldn't really see what was going on around them, and in between takes I nipped over and inflated the bladder. The first time I did it there was a little titter from Sigourney. I then deflated it, and then gently inflated it again and sensed a little movement.

'John, are you okay?' Sigourney asked the stuntman.

A little giggle was followed by a, 'Fine thanks, Sigourney.'

We kept this going for about an hour, and neither of them ever found out until much later what was going on, but it did cause some amusement for Jim and the crew!

As well as building the power loader, we also built the various guns, and with Hydroflex camera arms, we mounted two big MG 42 German machine guns, which looked really futuristic. BAPTY (film armourers) converted the largest bore blank-firing weapons they had and worked with us to create the hardware for the film. We even looked at putting strobe lights at the end of the barrels to light the actors, but they never really worked – the flash was so quick that the camera shutters often closed at the precise moment they flashed and missed them. We also built flamethrowers and worked very closely with Stan Winston who was designing the aliens because, for example, when we did the scene where the Alien Queen tears Bishop the robot in half – Stan made the Queen and two body halves of the dummy – we made a bayonet fitting that held it together until it was twisted. I put wires around the body and with a bungee-rubber rig on each wire and when pulled, it twisted the body and tore it apart looking as if the Queen had actually done it. Stan's team added the circuitry and 'milky' fluid.

We also did a lot of the effects in camera at Pinewood including quite a lot of work blowing up the models and crashing the dropship.

The robot welder which I managed to hire from a company here in the UK wasn't a prop but an actual working machine, complete with the plasma cutter. It was the first time I'd ever seen one. We programmed it to cut through the spaceship door which we built using ¼in steel plate; it was like a knife cutting through butter and at the time I thought it looked really great.

I guess we shot for four months or so, and I was delighted when all of our hard work paid off with Oscar and BAFTA nominations for Best Special Effects.

An American company called LA Effects were originally employed to supervise the visual effects on the movie, headed by Suzanne and Larry Benson. They'd budgeted the film's requirements and, at Jim's request, brought in the Skotak brothers – Dennis and Robert – who had worked with Jim on *The Terminator* – both really clever guys. About halfway through the shoot, it became obvious that the production was exceeding the VFX budget and consequently LA FX left the film and Brian Johnson came on to work along with Bob and Denny.

What complicated matters down the line was a clause in LA Effects' contract of employment which stated that should the film be nominated for an Effects Oscar, one of them would be a nominee – and that was regardless of whether or not they finished the picture.

When Academy Award night came around we had agreed that if we won, Stan would make the main speech and I would follow with a few thank yous, then Bob and Suzanne could add a word or two if time allowed. It was all a bit of a surreal experience especially being presented with the awards by Captain Kirk and Mr Spock, a.k.a. William Shatner and Leonard Nimoy.

It was my first nomination, and my first win. It was nice to win first time out as it meant on the other five occasions I was nominated and didn't win, I wasn't quite so disappointed.

Full credit to Jim. It was certainly one of the few sequels that was better than the original. Stan Winston became a great mate and when he rented a house just up the road from where I was living in London, we saw each other quite often.

Did winning an Oscar help my career? It certainly didn't harm it, but the phone didn't start ringing off the hook with massive offers. I did however keep myself very busy for the next decade or so pretty much without a holiday, so in that respect it was a lucky talisman.

CHAPTER 11

FURTHER BONDING AND ARGENTINA

James Bond came back into my life, albeit with a new look as Timothy Dalton – the fourth actor to play 007 – in *The Living Daylights* (1987). The production had actually started off with Pierce Brosnan picking up the famous Walther PPK, but his TV show *Remington Steele* was resurrected at the last possible moment, thus making it impossible for him to become Bond – for now.

They tested a whole array of actors including Sam Neill – but I think I may have scared him out of becoming Bond! My father had died about six months earlier and I had started clearing out his workshop in Greenford when I uncovered a drum of magnesium powder, still with the original seal on the neck of the bag inside. I rang up a chemist friend who ran a firework company and asked him the best way to dispose of it.

'Take it up the Pinewood backlot and bury it,' he helpfully suggested. I didn't think it a particularly good idea as at some point in the years ahead, someone would undoubtedly be constructing a set there and it could go shooting up into the air. It was then that my chemist friend suggested I burn it.

Being on the safe side I took a little of the magnesium out, placed it on a brick and held a blowtorch over it. Eventually, it started burning – perfectly fine and quite tame just like magnesium ribbon at school. I then took the whole drum over to Pinewood's backlot, took out a kilo or so and laid it in a long strip. I then set light to it using a propane torch – it didn't burn so much as explode. It set me alight from head to foot; I rolled around in a puddle of water in an attempt to extinguish it. Believe me, it was terrifying and really scary. I staggered from the lot towards the studio offices and the first-aid station, when a guy came running over shouting, 'You're on fire!' I realised my coat was ablaze and watched as he grabbed a stick, hoisted it off my back and threw it far away from us. I watched the burning jacket go up into the air and, as if in slow motion, head straight into the magnesium drum. I screamed, 'Get away, get away,' as loud as my lungs could manage. The resulting explosion was heard miles away and nearly took out half the windows at Pinewood.

I staggered into the first-aid department where they plunged my hands straight into a bowl of cold water before pouring water all over me whilst they phoned for an ambulance. I rang my girlfriend Trudie and asked her to come over, and then my mum – downplaying it as 'a bit of an accident' – and told her I was off to hospital, acutely aware that my father had suffered a very similar incident when he was a young technician. As the ambulance arrived, they led me out and looking at my hands in the bowl of water, the studio nurse said, 'You can't take that bowl – it's the property of Pinewood!'

My reply as you can imagine is not repeatable!

There was a bit of commotion with sirens and shouting and producer Nigel Wool in his office opposite asked his secretary Laura what was going on. She said, 'It looks like someone has been badly injured.'

'Anyone we know?' he asked.

'I don't think so, I think it's a Pakistani man.'

I was absolutely black, and all my hair had scorched – I was in hospital for ten days with bad second-degree burns.

A few weeks later, needing some light relief, I called director John Glen and asked if I could visit the team and watch the auditions. I arrived, still looking pretty grim and with lots of bandages on various parts, and John being the prankster he is said, 'Let me introduce you to Sam Neill,' and he took me over to a rather bemused Sam, who looked me up and down – I'd have been perfect casting for the invisible man can I tell you – when John proudly said, 'This is our special-effects expert.'

The look on Sam's face said it all – I don't think he wanted the job after that!

John Glen still laughs about it to this day!

By the way, I did call my chemist friend who said, 'I can't understand it, but leave it with me.' He worked out that as the magnesium was so old, some of it had decomposed into an oxide and that mixed with the remaining magnesium formed a flash powder – it's very vicious and people don't realise how dangerous it is. It can detonate exactly the same as high explosive.

Timothy Dalton was finally announced as our new star and filming got underway in Gibraltar, Morocco, Austria and the UK, including Pinewood. All the snow scenes were filmed on an ice lake in Weissensee, where you might remember the Aston Martin ended up after a chase with some police cars and cut a circle in the ice? We actually had to drive across the lake each morning to where we were filming, and I can still hear the noise of the ice cracking as we moved over it. One evening one of the safety guys was clearing some fresh snowfall off the ice with a bulldozer and dropped straight through it – fortunately in a shallow area. He did admit that the water was rather cold though!

Aston Martin had a promotional tie-up with the movie – the first since George Lazenby's film in 1969 – and people ask me, 'Were the gadgets and gags in the car all scripted or did you just come up with them?' They were indeed all scripted and storyboarded, long before the cars came into my workshop.

But we did get to have some fun designing a ski-cello case – we adapted a strengthened case with custom skis and a steering mechanism – for Tim and leading lady Maryam d'Abo to make their escape across the border.

It was then on to warmer climes as the unit moved to North Africa. John Glen had an idea of a little gag with a flying carpet. It wasn't one of his better ideas – and an absolute bugger to make look good as we essentially had Bond running across rooftops in Tangier and then jumping onto a rigid carpet which was spread across two cables at a 30° angle. It was cut out of the film in the edit.

Towards the end of the movie there was to be a huge bridge explosion, thanks to Bond dropping a bomb from the back of a Hercules plane, thus helping good guy Kamran Shah (Art Malik) and his men gain an important victory over the Soviets, in what was a slightly more serious Bond story with just one Bond girl – being mindful of the HIV/Aids-awareness campaigns – centred around a Russian defector, a shady American arms dealer and lots of double-crossing.

We had found a bridge for the sequences which involved men riding across on horseback, tanks crossing, and the Hercules flying over it. But the bridge itself was only 8ft above the riverbed and not the 'crossing with a huge ravine' as described in the script. I devised a foreground miniature and we set it up in the riverbed away from the action. Once it was lined up it fit perfectly with the bridge – the handrail and everything above it was real, but below the handrail was the model and it gave the impression the bridge was actually 200ft high. The 'river' was in fact just a bit of painted cling film and I found that we could pan and tilt the camera as long as the nodal point of the lens was in the centre of the camera head – a nodal pan which meant that there wasn't a perspective shift as the camera moved. We even got a bit more daring and threw in a zoom which we just about got away with. Doing moves like that does add to the reality and people just don't question it, they accept it for real.

There were other model sequences with the Hercules taking off and the Russian plane landing underneath it as it lifts. We required Bond's POV of the plane flying towards him so we put the camera on top of the camera car, but someone had to stay with it as it drove up the runway towards the very low-flying plane. As usual I was the only one silly enough to do it. I watched through the camera as the plane went over and it certainly looked fine to me, but the boys reckoned the landing gear was either side of my head as it flew past.

Across the Strait of Gibraltar, we filmed the exciting opening sequence on the Rock itself. It set up the storyline really, when two 00-agents were assassinated and a 'Smiert Spionem' (Death to Spies) message was found on their bodies. The assassin made his escape in a Land Rover with Bond hot on his heels, and Bond managed to get onto the roof and then inside – just as it drives off the side of the Rock and explodes mid-air. Bond was to pull out moments before, with his parachute opening.

The aerial stunt guys said, 'We'll shove the Land Rover out of the back of a plane with us on the top and you film it.'

I suggested it would be safer to take a helicopter up with a Land Rover hanging underneath which could be released by a trip switch with a camera in another helicopter. We built a lightweight Land Rover, sent it out to the Mojave Desert where we hauled it up through 10,000ft with a stuntman on top of it. Initially it was swaying about quite a bit, but once it settled and the stuntman pulled the release lever, the vehicle dropped like a ton of bricks. He managed to stay in place somewhat awkwardly for a short while before letting go, but the parachute cameraman was nowhere near. There wasn't much left of it after it hit the ground; it was as flat as a pancake but it did make a lovely noise when it hit!

We reverted to firing the car, with a dummy on its roof, from Beachy Head – and included a parachute release on a wire so as the car got X-ft away from the cliff, it pulled the parachute out cuing us to set off a radio-controlled explosion. Once cut together with live-action footage it worked really well.

An unexpected highlight of the filming was when we had a royal encounter in Q Branch. It was announced that Prince Charles and Princess Diana were going to visit the production and perhaps you'll recall one of the gags the Quartermaster showed off to 007 was his new 'ghetto blaster' which launched a missile? We set up a demo and explained to Prince Charles how it worked and invited him to press the buttons – the first fired the rocket – and then the second set off the explosion as it hit its target. He pulled both switches with split-second accuracy. Diana was at his side and just before HRH pressed fire, I made a comment to her about loud bangs. I think the picture taken at the time says it all.

Willow (1988) was a fantasy film brought to life by director Ron Howard and producer George Lucas.

Willow himself was a diminutive farmer who helped protect a special baby from a tyrannical queen who vowed to destroy her. There were a lot of effects – fires, smoke, arrows flying in the air – plus an underwater sequence that I don't think made it into the film, with a model of a huge fish – almost shark like – that Warwick Davis (who played the titular lead) discovered. Nick Dudman built the fish and we built a hydraulic rig to mount it on and installed it in the Pinewood water tank but sadly I don't remember seeing it in the final edit.

We then set off for location work in New Zealand. I'd actually just been in LA for the Oscars, and had flown back to London to change, repacked and the very next day flew off again – I didn't know which way was up. From Auckland we flew up to Queenstown and then hopped in a car for a two-and-a-half hour drive up a dirt road, followed by climbing up a mountain. It was a terrific location and you felt that you could see all the way to the South Pole.

A few days later it had snowed heavily overnight, and we were halfway up the dirt road the following morning when the road literally turned to sheet ice. The unit trucks and cars started sliding sideways and a bus in front of me locked its wheels and slid backwards straight towards me. Thankfully I managed to reverse out of its path as the bus slid by and it fortunately came to a stop just before the edge where it was a straight drop down several hundred feet. The production had to arrange helicopters to fly up, collect the vital crew members and take them on to the location whilst the roads were cleared by snow ploughs for everyone else to follow. It wasn't what you'd call easy access, that's for sure.

I started chatting with Ron and George about upcoming scenes.

'You know that sequence where you have a great big, impenetrable green hedge?' I asked, 'with a ring of fire that the heroes all jump through?'

'Yeah?' replied Ron.

'Wouldn't it be more interesting if it was a big wall of fire with a small green ring they jump through?'

'Can you do it?' he asked.

I had talked myself into a corner, but we managed to rig it up – it wasn't CGI back then and opticals were certainly more difficult. That technology didn't really begin to come to the fore until the 1990s with *Jurassic Park.* What George Lucas and Industrial Light and Magic (ILM) did with *Star Wars* was to bring in computer-controlled camera movement, which gave much better repeatability, particularly in model scenes. I'm not anti-CGI; it is a wonderful tool if used properly and when necessary. It puts films into a digital state and it certainly made green-screen work much, much better with a clearer separation and with better colour balance and light control – but it shouldn't be the automatic answer to everything!

Licence to Kill (1989) was Timothy Dalton's second Bond adventure and, as it turned out, his last. It had been decided very early in pre-production that the movie would be based in Mexico, far away from 007's traditional Pinewood home; unfavourable UK tax and a cheaper Mexican spend were the driving factors along with a largely South American set storyline of revenge, drug dealing and Bond's licence to kill being revoked. I know they said it saved money by relocating, but in my opinion what it actually did was make everyone work a lot quicker because we wanted to get out and get back home! That in turned saved some dollars from the bottom line. Mexico was fine as a base – we had great fun there and I couldn't really fault the Mexican crews – but in hindsight I think we all would have preferred Pinewood.

As the altitude of Mexico City was pretty hard on people it was decided that Cubby would not spend much time with us, but Barbara, his daughter was now rising fast and taking over the mantle. Barbara has always been a close friend and is always great fun to have around. She is a hard worker like her dad and has so many of his great qualities.

In line with Timothy's wish to take Bond back to the Ian Fleming books, with a slightly more serious and darker edge, there were not as many gadgets or gimmicks – yes he had a signature gun, and yes he had some explosive toothpaste, but there was nothing particularly outlandish.

One of the biggest sequences we were involved with featured a big tanker chase through the Rumorosa Pass, a winding stretch of road about 50 miles west of Mexicali, just over the border from California. It all ended – as all good Bond films do – with lots of explosions. Tim was great as he was always willing to get involved and do as much as he could for real. Health and safety was still a few years away back then. Tim ran from one of our biggest explosions himself and emerged from it to see off bad guy, Franz Sanchez (Robert Davi) by setting him on fire – necessitating stuntman Paul Weston to step in for a full-body burn in quite a gruesome and gritty despatch for a Bond baddie.

Model-unit work included firing a blazing pickup off a cliff whilst leading lady, Carey Lowell's plane went underneath. A very tricky model shot because we had to find a cliff we could access near a road straight enough that Nigel Brackley could take off and land the model from. After a long search we found one and just managed to get the shot but timing it was very difficult, especially with the camera turning at 120 frames a second to slow the action down.

Further location work took place in Key West, Florida with the submarines and diving work going on. The opening sequence was based around Felix Leiter and Bond intercepting villain Sanchez in a mid-air hijacking of Sanchez's plane. This meant we had to rig the plane hanging vertically under a helicopter with the propeller still turning. To do this we had to install a microlight engine (it was the only one light enough that would still work at any angle, even upside down) into the lightened and empty body of the plane, and as long as the helicopter didn't fly too fast, causing the plane underneath to feather, it worked fine.

After his arrest, Sanchez was being transferred to high-security prison by road but, wouldn't you know it, he gets sprung when the truck he is in swerves off the Seven Mile Bridge into the sea below. Someone stepped up and said, 'We'll just drive it over.'

'I don't think so! You'll kill yourself,' was my reply.

We rigged the armoured truck with radio-controlled steering and acceleration, whilst taking out a section of the handrail on the bridge, replacing it with a dummy one. One of my guys practiced the remote driving to make sure that it worked, but on the day of filming he wasn't very well so I had to take over at the last minute. How could I be sure I swerved the truck off the road at the right moment? Easy – I stood in the middle of the road right in front of it, and before it hit me, I had to veer it off – making sure I had the remote control the right way up!

When they later pulled the truck out of the water, the windscreen had dislodged on impact and decapitated the dummy in the driver's seat. Imagine if that had been a stuntman!

John Glen asked me to do a bit of splinter-unit work with actor Wayne Newton, who played Professor Butcher, a TV preacher who was in fact Sanchez's TV sales-man for drugs; he operated out of the 'Olimpatec Meditation Institute' which was in fact the Otomi Ceremonial Centre, Toluca, Mexico. Of course, I had to blow it all up at the end!

The film was quite notable for another reason – I first met my (now) wife Rosie on it. Halfway through shooting we were both sent home to the Hospital for Tropical Diseases in London suffering with amoebic parasites – thanks to dodgy Mexican food – though after ten days, we were able to return to set where love blossomed. We've been together ever since.

I got along very well with Tim Dalton and there's no doubting he's a very fine actor, but to be fair he had a less than perfect script as there was a writers' strike (the Writers Guild of America) called, which prevented long-time 007 screenwriter Richard Maibaum from completing his work.

Following the release of *Licence to Kill* there was a hiatus with the Bonds that lasted five or six years, all over a dispute with MGM's new owners selling TV rights at a knock-down price. As well as being grim for Bond fans, it was a pretty grim time for filming in the UK as a whole, and Pinewood was pretty deserted. But in happier news, Rosie and I moved in together – and wondered how we might now afford the rent!

I literally bumped into producer Ted Lloyd in the Pinewood bar, one of the remaining few busy areas of the studio, and he asked what I was up to.

'Nothing much,' was my understated reply. 'How about you?'

'Well I have this film, but you wouldn't be interested as it's too small ...'

'Who says I wouldn't be interested? What is it?' I asked.

He explained it was an adaptation of *Treasure Island* (1990) to be directed by Fraser Heston and starring his father Charlton. It wasn't exactly big budget but included six weeks location work in Jamaica – what's not to like about that, I wondered?

I read the script and noted there'd be lots of explosions, including muskets and cannons and we'd need to fix up some descender rigs for the actors/stuntmen falling out of the rigging when they were shot – it was nothing too complicated and that, with six weeks in Jamaica, led to me asking, 'Where do I sign?'

My favourite memory of the movie was with Charlton Heston, or Chuck as he was known, playing Long John Silver. This of course necessitated him losing a leg – well having it hidden from sight. He wasn't a method actor! The production team were a little worried about how he'd cope with it strapped up for hours on end and if he'd be okay to move around on a crutch; Chuck was getting on in years and had fallen off a lot of horses in his time and couldn't afford to topple over and break any

Russell Mulcahy

more bones. I said we'd build him a harness with a quick release and if he started feeling uncomfortable or unsteady, he could flick the release and his leg would drop down.

On the first day of shooting, Chuck walked onto the set of the Admiral Benbow Inn with a parrot on his shoulder, giving it all the 'Ahhh, Jim lad ...' dialogue. As the door swung open and Chuck hobbled in, the parrot bit his ear – Chuck swung round quickly, lost his balance, made a grab for the release but missed it completely and went flying backwards in the most unintentionally comic manner. Fortunately, he was not hurt but it did cause some muffled titters!

Then *Highlander II: The Quickening* (1991) came along. Line producer Chris Chrisafis mentioned it was going to be filmed in Argentina, which I must admit appealed to me more than the script, although I had seen the first *Highlander* film and quite enjoyed it. Rosie and I duly flew to Buenos Aires and started setting things up with director Russell Mulcahy and director of photography Phil Meheux.

William Panzer and Peter S. Davis, the main producers who had also been behind the first film in the franchise, were not particularly renowned for paying in a timely fashion, though I'm sure Sean Connery had his money banked before he even stepped on a plane. When they asked if any of the crew would like to move into an apartment rather than a hotel – no doubt thinking it would be cheaper – I said yes, as I've always found life is so much more pleasant in your own flat, particularly if it's going to be months away from home. They took us to a top-floor apartment, with balconies on three sides, overlooking La Recoleta Cemetery where Eva Peron is buried, the River Plate and the Alvear Palace. It was absolutely beautiful with a private lift and positioned right next door to the best hotel in town.

I noticed there wasn't any linen or bedding, pots and pans or kitchen utensils and mentioned it to the production office. 'Just buy it and give us the bill,' they told me. So, we bought everything brand new, and enjoyed nine wonderful months there!

However, about eight weeks into preparation, the producers ran out of money. They seemed pretty sure that further funding would be forthcoming as they had an insurance completion bond – which would guarantee the film would continue. Whilst they were negotiating a way forward, they suggested we could either stay put and they'd pay our accommodation and per diem living expenses – but no salaries – or

alternatively would fly us home. Quite a few did return home, grumbling all the way to the airport, but Rosie and I decided to stay, partly because – unbeknown to Rosie – I'd arranged for her mother and husband to fly out for a surprise visit and was keen to spend some time with them. Plus for $100 you could buy an airline ticket that would take you to any five cities in Argentina; we splashed out and, starting from Buenos Aires, flew to El Calafate, then up to the mountains, across glaciers, down to Ushuaia (the most southerly town in the world), then on to the penguin and sea-lion colonies, before ending up in Iguaza.

The producers got things back on track, though the completion-bond company had installed their own production people who were now taking a great interest in everything and for some reason always came to me with questions. In fact, we became good friends and when I was thinking of relocating to LA, they were hugely helpful in getting all my paperwork sorted for visas and getting work.

Whilst we were there, Rosie and I were invited to an evening soiree at the American Embassy to watch and celebrate the Oscar ceremony taking place in Los Angeles. The only people we knew when we arrived were Chuck Heston and his wife who we had just left in Jamaica and we spent the evening chatting to them and trying to see if there were any microphones hidden in the flower arrangements on the buffet table.

I should mention that when we landed in Argentina, the Austral was 600 to the US dollar. Three months later it was over 6000 to the dollar. I had a cash float, for purchases and equipment, in both local currency and in dollars – I always spent the pesos first and hung on to the dollars for as long as possible and at one point I had $30,000 which made me an Argentine millionaire! Our per diems were also paid in dollars and knowing our old producers well, most of the crew insisted on being paid cash every week, and each week I shot off to the American Express office to swap my dollars for traveller's cheques.

I had a lovely local assistant named Tom Cundom who had been a helicopter pilot during the Falklands conflict and he kindly arranged to take me to the government munitions factory with my explosives shopping list to see some tests and pick up what we needed. It beats going to Waitrose for the weekly shop! We were still technically at war with Argentina at that point and when the guys started bringing the explosives out to test, many of them misfired, some didn't go off at all and the staff ended up setting fire to the grass right in the middle of the explosives warehouses!

'It's not hard to see how we won, is it?' I quipped to Tom quietly. Thankfully he shared my sense of humour.

Argentina is a fabulous country and we made some really good friends there, though I think it's safe to say we had far more fun making the movie than anyone ever did watching it. Russell Mulcahy reportedly disliked the final cut so much that he walked out of the world premiere after just fifteen minutes. Someone said that it was rated as 'one of the worst films ever made' but I saw it and whilst it wasn't great it wasn't that bad. I recently watched the Director's Cut on DVD and I thought the flying sequences looked great, especially considering we had to hide the wires and rigs as there was no CGI to call on back then.

With work looking continually thin on the ground in the UK, Rosie and I decided to make our move to LA in search of new ventures. By happy coincidence John Glen was busy preparing *Aces: Iron Eagle III* (1992) in Arizona and it coincided with my US work permit coming through, many thanks to Gabe Videla of Special Effects Unlimited in Hollywood. Happily, that enabled me to join John on the film to supervise all the effects and models. The storyline involved pilot Charles 'Chappy' Sinclair (Louis Gossett Jr) discovering a drug-smuggling scheme at his own airbase, with an added subplot involving a local mayor whose daughter is kidnapped by a drug runner in Peru. Chappy decided to fly there with his friends – who all piloted performing Second World War aeroplanes – to free them. They flew a Spitfire, a North American T-6 Texan modified to resemble a Mitsubishi A6M Zero, a P-38 Lightning and a P-51 Mustang painted to resemble a Messerschmidt Bf 109. We also had four Soko G-2 Galeb aircraft painted to resemble Peruvian Air Force fighters. The prototype Scaled Composites ARES model was used to resemble the semi-fictional Messerschmitt Me 263 (which was designed and tested but never flew on its own power). It isn't the greatest film you'll ever see but it was well made and looked good on screen.

The planes had to do all sorts of stunts and gags and the only way of achieving it all economically and safely was with models; I was fortunate to be able to recruit Tad Krzanowski who had worked with me on some of the Bonds and was a brilliant model maker. He was then based in San Francisco where he'd been doing a lot of work with Lucasfilm. There was also Bob Wilcox, an electrical genius and model maker supreme who I had first met on *Raise the Titanic*. As the main unit filmed in and around Tucson, I rented an airfield near the border in Nogales to film all our sequences and purchased one of the old model Hercules planes we'd used on *The Living Daylights* from Eon and converted it to be the C123 aircraft that we blew up. We had some pretty big explosions and it was a good introduction to working in America.

The film was also memorable for introducing me to American effects technician Rick Thompson; we hit it off and went on to form a partnership, working together on a number of subsequent pictures including a Bond and several Harry Potters.

I next received a call to meet director Ron Howard (again) and producer Larry DeWaay with a view to working on the Tom Cruise/Nicole Kidman film *Far and Away* (1992) which was setting up part of its shoot in Ireland. As soon as we finished on *Aces*, Rosie and I shipped out to Dublin to start work on what was an epic American romantic-adventure movie with Cruise and Kidman playing Irish immigrants seeking their fortune in 1890s America. Dublin doubled for Boston and all the interiors were filmed at Ardmore Studios. There'd already been some location filming in Montana ahead of the unit arriving on the Emerald Isle.

Tom Cruise was perfectly lovely, but we had instructions not to make eye contact with him as he apparently didn't like it. I think it was more his minders and managers saying that, as it's not only impossible but rather stupid to think key crew members couldn't engage with the star and look at him as they spoke.

Out in Dingle, we had a helicopter set up with the Spacecam filming low passes across the sea, over the coast and up the cliffs on to a village where we were all hiding away in the houses making smoke come out the chimneys. We'd done three or four takes and set up for another, but the helicopter never arrived and no one could reach it by radio; we realised it must have gone down. I had a Range Rover 4x4 and grabbed a rope, a couple of my guys, and drove down dirt tracks to where the helicopter was coming in from, and as we got close we saw it sinking into the sea with the pilot and camera operator bobbing about in their life jackets. A couple of us waded in; the rocks were so slippery and slimy with seaweed plus it was freezing cold, but thankfully we managed to drag them out to await an ambulance. No one was seriously hurt, thank goodness.

The ambulance arrived and duly drove the two guys away along the track, but by this time some journalists had started arriving and one of them purposely blocked the ambulance in a stupid attempt to get a photograph. We all shouted at him to move but he ignored us, so I marched over and helped him into the ditch at the side of the road. My crew, realising there were more journalists arriving, dragged me away and drove me off before anyone got a photo of me. Mind you, I don't regret my actions.

One of the bigger models was of the boat taking our stars from Ireland to their new life in America across the Atlantic. Ron Howard said he thought they'd film it on the Pinewood tank but I suggested we could do it there in Ireland much better by building a large-scale model, taking it out into Dublin Bay where we'd have real sea, real sky, and real background. My mate Mike Turk sourced a riverboat hull of the correct shape and installed an engine, and a model builder near Dublin built the superstructure whilst my team made some moving figures to place on the deck – and that's the shot you see in the movie.

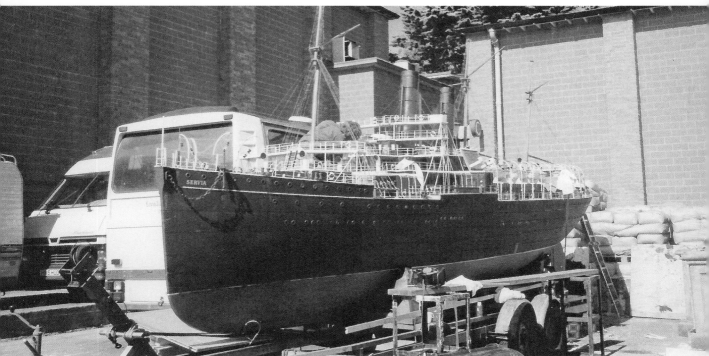

CHAPTER 12

COLUMBUS, CLIFFHANGER AND A BIT MORE BOND

1492 marked the arrival of western civilisation in the Americas when Christopher Columbus discovered the continent by accident – he was actually looking for a westward sea passage to the Orient. The 500th anniversary of his landing seemed ripe for a film biopic. There were in fact three released in 1992: *1492 – Conquest of Paradise, Carry On Columbus* and *Christopher Columbus: The Discovery*. The latter was directed by my old pal John Glen and produced by the Salkinds of *Superman* fame. I think John had inadvertently stepped into a bit of a problematic production, as another director had left – along with the proposed stars – when the Salkinds slashed the budget from $40 million to $8 million. But we're all wiser in hindsight.

  John asked if I would be free to join the film and explained there were a lot of marine requirements and that they had a genius whiz kid on the movie who knew everything about boats, and to be fair he knew quite a lot about rigging and boats of the period, but seemingly knew little about keeping film boats afloat; he'd used steel oil drums with aluminium caps as flotation and the steel, aluminium and salt water reacted causing the caps to leak and the ships started sinking! So one of my first jobs was to stabilise them and get them afloat again.

Production started off in Madrid, but no sooner had we arrived than news filtered down that funding was 'coming in slower than anticipated' (should I have appeared surprised?), so we shifted to Malta to keep things bobbing along with a small team working on the ships and second-unit requirements in early December 1991, whilst the Salkinds ran about looking for the money to keep us all afloat. Santa was obviously kind to them that year as after Christmas, the whole production flew out to the Virgin Islands whilst second unit director Arthur Wooster sailed across the Atlantic with his camera crew on one of the full-sized ships the Spanish Government had loaned us, to get as many shots as he could on the way – the Salkinds liked to kill two birds with one stone, but I think it proved a bit of a rough ride for poor Arthur in more ways than one.

The cast included Tom Selleck, Georges Corraface, Robert Davi, Catherine Zeta-Jones, Benicio Del Toro and Rachel Ward, and following the earlier high-level dropouts, we heard Marlon Brando was on the verge of signing on as Tomas de Torquemada. Brando was getting on in years and though a great presence to have on set, and no doubt helpful to the distributors, he had trouble remembering his lines – just as he did on *Superman* – so it proved a bit of a challenge for John G.; in fact it was rumoured Brando only did the film to get money he was still owed from *Superman*. In fact, the entire crew were concerned about getting their weekly pay and demanded cash in hand. To solve that problem, Ilya Salkind's wife used to fly in from Switzerland every Friday with a large suitcase, from which Ilya paid most of the cast and crew in cash – a queue of people ran the full length of the hotel corridor every Friday evening. We all then deposited our salaries in the safety deposit boxes at the hotel – Rosie and I worked out there must have been a million dollars in the hotel reception at any one time. I didn't know if it was safer to leave our money there and wait for someone to twig and rob the lot, or hide it under the bed in our room and take our chances.

Stories then reached us about unpaid bills in Madrid, financial commitments to the Maltese government not being met and I later discovered several of my crew were not paid their final salary after leaving the location – same old, same old Salkinds.

The film flopped on release. I question whether taking on the picture did John Glen more harm than good; he came into it to help the producers out of a hole, yet found himself forever hamstrung by promised finance not being in place and budget reductions enforced across all departments and whilst John did an admirable job, had he received the proper support and budget he was promised, it would have been infinitely better.

Rosie and I then returned to the UK and had three weeks to arrange our wedding!

It was a wonderful day, filled with so many happy memories, and so many mates. Mike Turk and Phil Hobbs as my best men and that's when, at the reception in Rosie's father's converted barn, that Mike told the 'crabs' story in front of all the assembled guests!

An American effects man I knew named Bruce Steinheimer was working with Larry Cavanaugh on a Sylvester Stallone movie called *Cliffhanger* (1993), and though it was early days, they'd suffered a few setbacks and problems. Bruce was trying to deal with things pretty much on his own and was shooting up in the Dolomites when he asked me to join them, knowing I'd worked on the Fred Zinnemann picture in Switzerland and that I knew quite a bit about mountain safety, flying in and out in helicopters, and who the best guys were to have around.

Shortly after arriving, during my first day on top of a mountain, I heard bad weather was coming in, which would prevent any helicopters being able to reach the proposed location. As our only shelter would be two tiny tents, I asked what the Plan B was – and they didn't have an answer. That and a few other happenings made me feel very uncomfortable. I went to see Alan Marshall, the producer and told him I wasn't really prepared to work on any location that I wasn't able to ski out of.

'What you're saying, love, is that you're f-ing scared,' he replied.

'If you want to put it like that, then yeah, I am. But I also have to tell you your picture is in trouble because no one is sorting out how to do things.'

'What do you mean?' he asked.

'I've spent all my life working out how to achieve shots and sequences safely, and no one is doing it on this film,' I told him honestly.

'Well, will you work something out and present it to the director?' Alan asked.

I gathered all the storyboards together and went to visit all the locations; one was totally inaccessible as they'd closed the cable car for repairs! Anyhow I broke all the sequences down and laid out all the shots and where we might do each one, what the access was etc. I hadn't been introduced to Renny Harlin at this stage and so Alan asked that I take everything to the rushes screening that evening where at the end he said, 'Don't go everyone, John wants to make a presentation.'

Thrust centre stage, I cleared my throat and began to explain the issues and potential solutions.

Renny said, 'Finally I have someone on my picture who understands camera direction!'

Renny then started calling me on set for everything related to effects, which at times was a little embarrassing, but I was suddenly an important part of the crew and I was asked if I would continue to Cinecittà Studios in Rome to run the studio work. I agreed but with the proviso I wasn't replacing anyone on the American team.

Once Rome was completed, I was asked to fly to Colorado to have a look at the opening air-to-air transfer sequence which they were setting up to shoot there. One of the planes was a DC-9 with its tail cone removed so that when you stepped out of the cabin at the back you literally looked into thin air; the second aircraft was a Jetstar. Aerial coordinator Marc Wolf was working with stuntman Simon Crane and I suggested to them that we could build two capstan winches (which we did by taking the rear axle and motor off two golf buggies) and bolt one in each aircraft, and as the planes flew in formation, we could let the rope out the back of the DC-9 into the Jetstar and connect them both with the winches to transfer stuntman Simon out of the DC-9 and into the Jetstar.

We went up to test the idea at 16,000ft though at that time, I was told, no one had ever taken off in a DC-9 without a tail cone in position, and that was quite an experience. Then the DC-9 had to fly about just above stalling speed, with full flaps, and the stall alarm was sounding constantly but it was the only way the Jetstar could keep up and we could keep the planes together.

We then tried to get the rope out and across, but with turbulence and the Jetstar having two big jet engines at the rear, we were conscious that if we misjudged things even by a couple of inches it'd be goodnight and goodbye. It was just too dangerous so I suggested we try another way; have Simon tied to a rope and winch him out the back of the DC-9 and start the transfer between planes. Then VFX could add the other end of the rope into the Jetstar. We could then cut to a camera

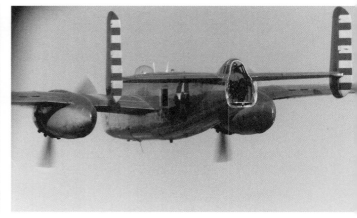

inside the smaller jet to see him come through the door. It meant that it would be done with more cuts, but it would be much safer and just as effective.

Off Simon went and when he reached the Jetstar, he bounced all over the fuselage and wing and got quite close to the engine, and I must admit I was terrified for him – he was fine though and parachuted to safety. Throughout the shot as I was paying the rope out with Simon on the end of it, I had a very sharp knife clenched between my teeth, to cut the rope just in case the planes became tied together by accident.

I then took a 'kicking dummy', so called because it's a dummy that kicks and moves as though alive, which was doubling for a pilot being thrown out of the plane. It was operated by compressed air and I sat on the edge where the tail cone used to be on the DC-9, my legs in the slipstream and the dummy on my lap listening to the pilot through my headphones.

'Clear underneath, go!' came the instruction, and with that I pulled the pin to start the dummy into action and pushed it out. Empty desert passed by below as I watched it fall but just as it was about to hit the ground, a little Indian dwelling came into view. Can you imagine a kicking, screaming dummy landing in your garden? We sent a helicopter out later to find and retrieve it, but they never found it.

Another scene using the kicking dummies required an avalanche plunging down a sheer cliff face in the Dolomites with a body. To do this we constructed a large 'Dump Box' to hang underneath a helicopter with two trapdoors; we filled it with fake rocks, a bit of fake snow and a kicking dummy in the middle. We then flew up and over the edge of a cliff face and once lined up and cameras rolling, I hit the release and everything fell out and all was caught on camera by a second helicopter and several cameras on the ground.

This time the helicopter that went off to find the dummy did bring it back. I had the Dump Box all filled up again with the rocks and snow just waiting for the dummy to arrive. Just as the helicopter with it arrived (it was painted as an orange medivac chopper) some German tourists pulled up and saw me drag the body out and run over and throw it into the Dump Box.

'Nein! Nein! Nein!' came a German man screaming at me across the car park. I guess he thought it was a real body.

I jumped in the helicopter and flew off!

A model of the Jetstar crashing had already been filmed in LA some weeks before, but Renny wasn't happy and asked my opinion. I agreed it didn't look authentic. Renny asked what we could do; I thought for a minute and suggested that we could build a model in a better, larger scale, landscape some scenery with a sky background in a parking lot out in the valley and shoot the plane crashing by using a rig to move it at high speed. We filmed with a very high-speed camera and lots of carefully placed powdered snow of the right size; we made it look quite spectacular. Simple, but effective. We also blew up the model of the DC-9 in the same place.

John —

Thank you for saving my movie. I couldn't have done it without you. And I mean it. RT

When *Cliffhanger* was nominated for an Oscar, I was proud to be one of the nominees. We didn't win, but it was a great picture with great challenges and I think the moral of working on the film was you don't have to endanger yourselves and hang from fingernails; you can achieve things safely and much easier.

The Ghost in the Machine (1993) was next on my CV. It was an American science-fiction film about a serial killer who, after a car accident, has an MRI scan and a surge from an electrical storm causes his soul to be absorbed into the machine. It was directed by the lovely Rachel Talalay and also got me back together working with Rick Thompson again.

This was closely followed by a movie called *Love Affair* (1994). It was to star Warren Beatty and Annette Bening, directed by Glenn Gordon Caron – who turned out to be a big Bond fan. Warren Beatty (who was also one of the producers) invited me to meet him over lunch at a little restaurant at the top of Mulholland Drive, to talk about all the technical aspects and in particular boats and gimbals – which featured extensively. With my previous experience on *North Sea Hijack* (1980), I explained placing a boat and camera on a gimbal would be pointless as they'd just move together, losing the audience's static point of view. I suggested an easier and more economical way would be to construct a small set that we could make rock about, combined with little gimmicks, such as placing some glasses on a table that slid about, would be far more effective than building a 200ft-long boat. Warren looked at Andrew Davis (executive producer) who was also lunching with us and said, 'I told you the limey would know!'

Rick Thompson and our team joined me, and we all shipped out to the next location in Tahiti. On the first night, Warren arranged a few drinks to welcome everyone and when he arrived, Warren totally ignored me and went straight to my wife Rosie, picked up her hand and kissed it as he said, 'I've been dying to meet you Mrs Richardson.' Rosie has been a fan ever since!

I needed to do a bit of research on atolls for the model shoot that was to come later – so whilst we were filming on location in Tahiti and Moorea, they flew Rosie and me, on a private plane, to Marlon Brando's private atoll and we had the most marvellous day wading around in the lagoon and taking pictures of palm trees. How many people can say that? But reference is so important for models and someone has to do it. By the way, at the main airport in Tahiti, an Air France 747 had overshot the runway and was sitting in the sea – though someone from the company had been sent over to paint out the logo, to avoid any embarrassment!

From that location we went straight to New York where we filmed for a week or two, and boy what a change in temperature that was!

On return to LA we set about having our 747 model landing on a Pacific atoll in a storm. The 24ft-long miniature 747 aircraft was moved, as we had done in *Cliffhanger*, by towing it back and forth on a two-to-one purchase using a powerful American pickup truck. We covered our miniature atoll in sand and dressed it with little bendy palm trees and created a hurricane using large wind machines and a very fine water spray. We filmed it all in a car park out in the valley near LA. Another fun shoot that I thoroughly enjoyed.

*Crusade h*as often been mentioned in the list of 'best films never made'.

Producer Alan Marshall invited me to join the medieval epic, with Paul Verhoeven directing – apparently, he wanted the film to be controversial in tone from the outset. On the day I met Paul for the first time, for my 'interview', I had the most terrible cold and wasn't feeling at my best; that obviously came through in the meeting as it didn't go at all well, and I left feeling disappointed. Alan rang the next day to say as much, but I asked if we could do it again and happily, second time around minus the worst of my cold, everything clicked. I then had to be 'passed' by star Arnold Schwarzenegger – happily he accepted me too. Incidentally, the proposed supporting cast of the European-based epic included Jennifer Connelly, Gary Sinise and Charlton Heston, and the reported budget was $100 million – so it was certainly a big picture.

Norman Reynolds was engaged as production designer, whilst I set up my workshop at Pinewood before heading off on a recce to Alicante, Spain, and then up into the Pyrenees mountain range. In the middle of it all, Renny Harlin asked me to work with him on his next film, *Cutthroat Island* (1995) – which of course, sadly I had to decline.

I then came down with chickenpox and had to take a little time off and when I returned, the financing studio Carolco decided to pull the plug on the movie. I think they realised things were going over-budget, even at this early stage, and they got the jitters. Though ironically, they then fully financed Renny's *Cutthroat Island* to the tune of $100 million (and lost their shirts on it) whilst I ended up without a job!

I had heard that Eon were setting up their next Bond film, *Goldeneye*, so gave them a call, but discovered they'd already taken on Derek Meddings to oversee the model work, so I returned to LA with my tail between my legs.

As luck would have it, *Bushwhacked* (1995), a comedy starring Daniel Stern came along and following that, *The American President* (1995), with a big starry cast including Michael Douglas, Annette Bening, Martin Sheen and Michael J. Fox. Location filming was to be in Washington, so one of the first things we had to do was visit the White House. Annette had arranged to meet us – director Rob Reiner, the producers, production designer and little me on a corner opposite for lunch, after which we had an amazing tour of the White House; Clinton wasn't in residence but we met his vice president, Al Gore, and got to see the Oval Office, all the corridors, the downstairs bunker where the Secret Service are based and the tunnel that goes directly across to the Treasury. The script called for mist outside and it was laughingly suggested that I'd be the first Englishman to put smoke over the White House since independence.

Then came *Broken Arrow* (1996) with John Travolta, Christian Slater and Samantha Mathis for director John Woo.

Sadly, it was a very unhappy picture for me. Producer Bill Badalato didn't really like me – he was one of those producers who surrounded himself with his favourites and as I wasn't a yes-man, I am afraid I didn't go down too well. I'd meet with John Woo for instance, who would tell me what he wanted, and then I'd hear from Mr Badalato, who contradicted everything John said.

'You're not doing it that way, you're going to do it this way ...' he barked.

My first loyalty on a picture is to the director, as he is the captain of the ship, and so the producer and I were very much at loggerheads. Then Badalato brought in a stuntman and another second unit director, who – whether John was aware or not I don't know – were essentially there to do things the producer wanted and to coerce John into his way of thinking. I tried to protect John as best I could, which annoyed Mr Badalato no end and so he fired me. I accepted the situation but said I'd stay on until my replacement arrived for the sake of keeping the picture going.

Three days went by and Mr Badalato called me in to say he realised I had a pretty good handle on things after all and asked me to stay on – what a turn-up for the books! We finished the movie and I don't mind admitting I couldn't wait to get away from the toxic atmosphere, but what upset me more than anything was the thought John Woo might have believed I was being difficult whereas I was actually fighting my corner for him and for the picture. The problem always with those situations is that you are never allowed to know the full story, but I still feel my actions were correct from what I knew at the time.

'In the distant future the Earth is at war with a race of giant alien insects, and so they sent for director Paul Verhoeven and *Starship Troopers* (1997) to save the day. Oh, and me. Location work was in Wyoming – not exactly the culinary centre of America. Our main set, the Starship Outpost, was built in Rattlesnake Canyon, and it wasn't called that without reason. It was primarily soft clay in the valley and every time it rained it was like a skating rink! Anyhow, there was to be a big explosion – perhaps one of the biggest ever – on what I can best describe as being a 'napalm run' over half a mile long. It was to be so big that we even warned air traffic control – which was just as well as one pilot in a jet 40,000ft up radioed it in. The fireball travelled at 300mph and was a mixture of petrol, kerosene, a lot of dynamite, oil drums, sandbags and about 10 miles of twin flex.

Back in Los Angeles we had a daily two-hour drive to a location in Orange County – a sort of futuristic firing-range set. I must admit it was a horrible set, which Paul hated and he didn't really know how he was going to set-up to film on it. In turn, I didn't know what to rig.

'What have you got prepared?' he asked me.

'What do you want?' I asked back.

Well, talk about lighting a touchpaper – Paul took out his frustration on me by shouting and yelling. As you've probably realised, I don't mind being told when I'm wrong, but I will not put up with anyone shouting and screaming at me when I've not done anything wrong.

I yelled back and called for producer Alan Marshall and told him I was quitting and he can tell that XXXX exactly what he can do with his movie!!! I then rang Rosie and said, 'We're looking for another job.'

I was on set the next day preparing to hand over to a new guy once they found one, when Paul walked on, grabbed my hand, dragged me into the centre, called all the crew together and said, 'I owe John an apology, it was my fault. I'm really sorry. It won't happen again – John please stay and finish the film.' We had a little hug and he was fine – for about three weeks. But we got through it. At the end of shooting, he took Alan Marshall and I and our respective wives to dinner, and at the end hugged me as though we were best of friends. Other people who have worked with him tell me he's like that – he means no malice, he just gets a bit upset! Life is too short to bear grudges though.

Having missed out on working on the previous Bond film, I was delighted to hear Pierce Brosnan's second adventure as 007, *Tomorrow Never Dies* (1997), was gearing up when Barbara and associate producer Tony Waye called, asking if I was available.

Roger Spottiswoode had been signed as the new director and was then in LA, so Tony suggested I went to meet him – we'd actually worked on *Straw Dogs* together so knew one another of old and talked about those times and the movie ahead. I got all my old model crew back together and this time, with Pinewood being fully booked, we were based at a converted factory in Frogmore, near Watford. Chris Corbould was looking after the physical effects and we obviously knew one another very well because he had worked on many films with me. There was lots of water-based action in the script, and I had to work out where we were going to shoot sequences with a Royal Navy frigate, and a stealth boat; we needed a big tank but I didn't think the one in Malta was big enough. I knew they'd just built a new tank in Rosarito in Mexico for *Titanic* (1997), which was in the final days of shooting. I went to meet production designer Peter Lamont and director Jim Cameron there, and was given a grand tour – it was perfect; deep enough for sinking, large enough for moving boats around and with a clear horizon. I met the tank supervisor, a chap named Charlie Arneson who was very helpful, and I also spoke to a couple of the UK construction boys who I knew from years gone by, and who had been working on *Titanic* and asked them to stay on for me. My old team, Bob and Tad up in LA agreed to build the 50ft frigate model there, whilst the stealth boat model was built in the UK and container-shipped out along with some inboard/outboard engines. Whilst south of the border I also smoothed the way for the unit by sorting out various contacts, places and shipping agents – I guess I put on a production hat which I actually really enjoyed. There was a tower crane spanning half the width of the tank which I thought we could use for a camera platform with a basket hanging underneath – I knew Roger loved camera movement and this would give me the ability to 'fly' over most parts of the tank.

The thing with a Bond, and now most other films, is that the premiere and release date is set long in advance of shooting, and quite often before a director signs up. Initially the script had centred on a villain who planned to destroy Hong Kong on the eve of the city's July 1997 transfer of sovereignty to China; however, the film's premiere was set for November 1997, so it would all be outdated and old news by then. They had to start 'almost from scratch at T-minus zero!' as Roger Spottiswoode put it. Bruce Feirstein came on board and wrote a new script about a media mogul becoming so powerful he could influence and even write the news – no matter the human cost. But Bruce was playing catch-up and we didn't have a completed script on the first day of filming, so rewrites were going on throughout which is always slightly worrying.

Rather than flog my crew to death, I managed to schedule our filming so we started work at noon or 2 p.m. each day, spent a while doing day shots before then prepping night shots, and we'd usually shoot until 11 p.m. – early enough to get everyone back to the hotel before the bar closed. Everyone was happy, and everyone was working at their very best.

In other 'business', we worked on models for the opening sequence, where Bond steals a jet – he flew it through a fireball whilst the jet pursuing him blew up. We also did a model for Bond's BMW flying off the car-park roof before Chris's live-action crew smashed it into the shop front.

An amusing thing happened as I was flying back to London after one recce early in the production, in Virgin upper class. I was having a drink at the bar when a young lady sat next to me and we started chatting; she mentioned she was flying to London for a screen test to be in the next Bond film.

'Oh really?' I enquired innocently.

We chatted for a while, but I never said anything about what I did and the very next day I walked onto the stage at Frogmore and saw her there.

'Hiya,' I called out.

Her face was an absolute picture. Sadly, she didn't get the part though; it went to Teri Hatcher.

Pretty much everything on the film was shot in camera and pretty much on schedule. The only real issue we had was getting pyrotechnics across the US/ Mexico border as there was one particular border guard who liked to make life difficult and Sod's Law dictated everything *had* to go through him. Eventually we got him tamed but it did cause all sorts of delays and aggravations.

Crossing the border at Tijuana was a nightmare, especially coming back into the USA. Our hotel manager managed to bag me an Executive Border Pass which was great until we discovered the queue at that post was even worse because they had given so many of these bloody passes out.

Tomorrow Never Dies was my first Bond film without Cubby Broccoli. I love his daughter Barbara to bits, and she's a fantastic producer and a great pal, but I missed Cubby's presence on set – I think I always will.

I had a second hip replacement after the movie and as I was recovering, so was Renny Harlin – from his adventures with pirates on *Cutthroat Island*. His next project was *Deep Blue Sea* (1999). Producer Duncan Henderson asked me to go in for a meeting and talked about the plotline: at an island research facility, Dr Susan McAlester (Saffron Burrows) is harvesting the brain tissue of DNA-altered sharks as a possible cure for Alzheimer's disease. Though of course things go wrong and the sharks take their revenge.

I was hired, but then the production went into hiatus pending rewrites – they kept me on and sent me on a scout back to Rosarito Studios to check things out

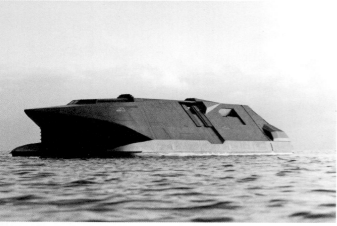

for the construction of an old wartime fort out at sea, which had been converted to the underwater research facility. They designed so as to shoot everything out to sea from the tank, and then proposed putting a blue screen on the reverse side to shoot the reverse shots, but the lighting cameraman was worried about shadows on the blue backing with the sun going round. The other concern that worried the producers was the cost of all the additional digital work that would be required.

'Can I say something?' I asked. 'The structure has four legs and a centre section, so it's pretty symmetrical, so why don't you shoot out to sea, then re-dress the set slightly for the reverses and shoot it out to sea once again – no one will know the difference.'

They looked puzzled for a moment, but then realised it would work.

Walt Conti from northern California built a mechanical swimming shark and it is amongst some of the best work I've ever seen. It weighed 2 tons and it could swim on its own, albeit with an umbilical cord. It could also be mounted onto a pole arm so it could be moved in and out, up and down and just about anywhere in the set. Unfortunately, it did have a nasty habit of just 'going off'; one day in a very small flooded set, it shot up in the air at lightning speed and nearly took my head off. You soon learned not to stand too close.

There was all the usual work you'd expect with a sea-based film: tip tanks emptying water all over the set, water hoses firing in, rain, storms, wind ... and explosions.

As we seemed to be more America-based now, Rosie and I bought a house in LA and any weekends we could get away we'd drive up, have a decent meal, do a bit of shopping and load up the car to drive back again. On the previous shoot in Rosarito for the Bond film, I had arranged a nice hotel for all the team with a golf course attached, which pleased quite a few of the guys. The manager was rather pleased because we spent so much time and money there and we were very happy

to find ourselves staying there again on this film. However I was rather embarrassed when I discovered that he'd put a plaque on the wall in my old room saying 'John Richardson stayed here – James Bond director'. If only! Fortunately, I convinced him to take it down before anyone saw it.

Funnily enough I went from Mexico straight onto another Bond, *The World Is Not Enough* (1999) with director Michael Apted at the helm. I'd worked with Michael on his first film, so it was a happy reunion. As mentioned, I was US-based so coming back to the UK had certain advantages – being 'foreign hire', I had a per diem (daily allowance), a flat in London, a car and a nice salary. Magic.

Happily, there was a lot of model work on the movie with boats, a 55ft-long submarine – which had to sit vertically – and be controlled remotely with the back end blowing off.

A 55ft-long submarine tilting on end meant we needed a 100ft-deep expanse of water – and where else do you go for that, but the Bahamas? A full flotation system was designed, and I went to a mini-sub workshop in Southsea who made us underwater electronics set up so we could control everything from one box. An underwater explosion is difficult especially with cast and crew members in the area, so we did it with compressed air and flashbulbs.

Complicating things a little, we had remora – a fish who follows bigger fish, and somehow seem to attach themselves to feed off the bigger ones – anyway this one thought the sub was a bigger fish. We couldn't get the damn thing away from us – every time one of the divers chased it away it kept coming back. It was quite hysterical. Also, we had an infestation of sea lice – the tiny parasites turn the water black and there's nothing you can do apart from waiting for them to move on.

The submarine model lay on the ocean floor quite a lot of the time, and whenever we broke for lunch, we tied it up securely to our mother ship, because 100ft further along the seabed there was a drop-off which I was told went down 1,000ft or more. One day I was sitting on the deck of our unit boat and suddenly wondered, 'Did the boys tie up?' I looked over the side down into the clear water below – the submarine wasn't where it should be and had broken off its wires and was slowly bobbing along the bottom towards the drop-off. Panic! You have never seen half a dozen guys get their diving gear on so quickly and get down to the bottom 120ft below. I reached the sub, dug my feet in the sand, tried to hold it whilst the boys brought ropes in. My blood ran cold imagining having to phone Barbara and say, 'We can't shoot any more as we've lost the sub.' However all was well and we lived to film it another day.

I oversaw a little live-action stuff there, of Bond swimming and in fact got one of our safety divers – who was a good double for Pierce Brosnan – to be 007 for an afternoon.

There were also several complex scenes to be shot above water: there were some helicopter miniatures with buzz saws flying over the caviar factory on the Pinewood backlot; Bond's BMW linking two live-action locations, by driving from one through to another terrain in Azerbaijan; the opening sequence hot-air balloon exploding on the Millennium Dome; the Q-Boat coming out of MI6 and into the River Thames with an explosion in the wall; an oil-pipeline miniature build in Black Park adjacent to Pinewood, which of course we blew up.

JR and Marcus rigging the balloon to blow up.

I also travelled to North Wales and Snowdonia with a splinter unit because there is a big water pipe there on the Electric Mountain (Dinorwig Power Station) – I took some stills and sent them to Michael Apted and he said, 'Can you do some moving shots for me?' We did it handheld out of the helicopter because we didn't have a proper helicopter mount with us; it's amazing what you can get away with. We also made a piece of the model pipeline blend in with the real one in the background; it looked great. It turned out to be one of Pierce's very best Bond films.

Ahead of my next outing with Commander Bond, I took on *The Family Man* (2000) a romantic comedy-drama from director Brett Ratner, starring Nicolas Cage and Tea Leoni.

Brett is totally hyperactive, but fun to work with! It was all fairly run-of-the-mill stuff but for the many snow scenes we had to cover large areas of Teaneck, New Jersey. I used an idea that I had used before and we modified a Honda snow thrower by adding a box onto the front and by feeding the magnesium sulphate that we used for snow into it; the blower distributed it smoothly, evenly and quickly over the ground. It certainly made the job easier and quicker even when the set dresser traipsed all over it as soon as we had finished, just to put up a wreath on the front door. The footprints ... so annoying!

A child magician then came into my life, but before we get to him, I should mention my last association with 007.

Martin Asbury, Lee Tamahori and JR on a model set

Bond was back. Oh yes, *Die Another Day* (2002) was cranking up production. Lee Tamahori was chosen as director for Pierce Brosnan's final outing and was an interesting choice.

The final script was still being worked on and a release date had been set. I must admit I struggled when I joined the movie because it pushed us more and more into CGI work, shooting models against a blue screen and then digitally adding things like smoke afterwards – I would have preferred to do more in camera but that was not possible given the requirements. For me, the best thing was being able to continue my working relationship with the wonderful Paul Wilson; he was one of the most experienced, talented and brilliant cameramen I've ever worked with.

I did live in the vain hope of Lee realising the visual effects were being pushed too far into the realms of computer gaming, but it wasn't to be. Personally, I hated the scene with Bond surfing across a tsunami – it did not look great and a few of us never expected it to.

I also had issues with the ice palace. It's one thing for me to create a model based on something that exists, but it's impossible to make a model look good if it cannot exist in the real world – the ice palace could not have been built out of ice; structurally it would have been totally unsound. I felt it lost the model some believability.

We did some good explosions sweeping across minefields and we filmed a model hovercraft going over a waterfall – probably the only things shot that I was truly satisfied with.

Invisible cars, aircraft breaking up mid flight and all the other stuff was very dependent on CGI. To me, I am afraid it didn't look as real as it should have.

A little part of my unhappiness probably stemmed from the fact I'd completed one *Harry Potter* film, and they asked me to do the second, but I was contracted to do *Die Another Day* by that point and asked if I could overlap. It caused me complete brain damage.

One film went over schedule, the other wasn't fully ready to start. I had two different crews, two different sets of headaches and not much more salary to show for it.

But I did feel uncomfortable about my work on the Bond movie and I think by the end, the producers knew they had to go back to basics. They had to reboot it all which they did brilliantly for *Casino Royale* (2006). I have nine Bonds on my CV, even if one was the Woody Allen version, and remain incredibly proud of them all.

CHAPTER 13

BROOMSTICKS AND MAGIC: PART ONE

I first became aware of the Harry Potter books when I was working on *The Family Man* in New York and heard a bit of the buzz about how this series of children's books was taking the bestseller list by storm. The third book in the series, *The Prisoner of Azkaban*, had just been published and that prompted me to buy a copy of the first book – *The Philosopher's Stone* – to see what all the fuss was about. I think I read it in one night – I was enthralled and it was exactly the sort of book I had wanted to read as a kid growing up, but could never find. Of course, I started visualising it as a film and thought it would be rather wonderful to be involved in this world of magic but went back to the day job.

Having wrapped on *The Family Man* we returned to LA and that's when Duncan Henderson got in touch – we'd worked together on *Deep Blue Sea* – to say he'd been signed as line producer on the first Potter movie – *Harry Potter and the Philosopher's Stone* (2001) – and asked if I was free to meet with him, producer David Heyman and executive producer Mark Radcliffe, and director Chris Columbus. I didn't need to think twice!

At the meeting we chatted about the first book, how it could translate to film and the main challenges of things such as making broomsticks fly. I became fairly animated and excited, and said I'd never seen a broomstick fly on screen with any believability before (not that I'd seen *that* many), and suggested a few ideas of how I'd approach it. The next thing I knew I was offered the job. Although we knew there were going to be seven books in the series – because J.K. Rowling said so – the producers never spoke of a series of films and I got the impression it was a case of 'let's see how the first one goes.'

We set up at Leavesden Studios in May 2000, but it wasn't anything like the studio you see there today – it was once a Rolls Royce factory until the Bond film *GoldenEye* (1995) took it over as a makeshift temporary studio when Pinewood proved unavailable. There were holes in the roof and the electrical wiring was fairly antiquated; I used to laugh walking down the corridors where there were white tape

lines – just like around a murder victim in police shows – which were in fact positions for bins to be placed when it started raining, to catch all the drips. They say film-making is glamorous!

For my part, I started by budgeting all the special effects, not only the broomsticks but all the physical effects throughout.

Chris Columbus was a great director and I really loved working with him – to my mind he set the whole style, structure, look and cast in place for the franchise and he deserves huge credit for that. Warner Brothers who were backing the film had suggested Steven Spielberg amongst others to direct and whilst I'm not sure of all the ins and outs, I believe that David Heyman and J.K. Rowling were keen to ensure that the story retained its Britishness, and Chris Columbus, having made the *Home Alone* movies, whilst not British, was the perfect choice to helm as he 'got' the British sensibilities and he was brilliant working with kids.

An open casting call was held to find the young children at the centre of the stories – Harry, Hermione and Ron. They needed to be around 9–10 years old and willing to commit to a possible series of seven planned book adaptations (which turned out to be eight), and of course it made all the news reports of the day when Daniel Radcliffe, Emma Watson and Rupert Grint were announced as the young leads. They were stars in the making!

Steve Kloves had written the screenplay and now, behind the camera, a great team was assembled including Stuart Craig to design the movie, Chris Carreras as first assistant director and the brilliant Nick Dudman was brought in to design the creature effects – that was a masterstroke as the make-up effects and magical animatronic creatures were amongst the best I'd seen.

Daily production meetings were held at Leavesden to discuss every single aspect of the script, usually in a room right up at the top of the building where we had frequent terrific brainstorming gatherings which made us all feel part of the creative process and it was partly because of that I feel the first two movies were possibly the most enjoyable to work on – for me at least.

Chris was concerned about how we might make the floating candles in the Great Hall work for real – they featured in the background of so many sequences, particularly in that first film; to CGI them throughout would have been hugely expensive and, like me, Chris was of the belief if we could do it for real it would look better. Of course, using wax candles was a no-no as they'd burn down and cause mayhem with continuity so after testing a few ideas out, I devised a way of using a large number of gimbals – that could be electronically controlled – from which we attached 300–400 'candles'. These were actually made from a nylon tube with a spirit well and wick inside. They stayed lit for a few hours without burning down and we hung them via fine tungsten wires – they literally floated in mid-air and Chris thought they looked amazing.

On his first day of filming as Professor Dumbledore – head of Hogwarts School where Harry, Hermione and Ron were enrolled – Richard Harris called for me to meet him on the Great Hall set. I wondered if there was a problem but to my great delight, he said he wanted to tell me how terrific he thought it all looked. I in turn reminded him of the laughs we shared on *Juggernaut*.

Though for all our planning what we hadn't bargained on was the British weather – when it rained or the wind got up, the holes in the roof and door of the stage became a major issue. The most horrendous drafts blew through the set and caused the candle flames to flicker and move; several meetings later, we decided the safest option was to take them down and CGI them after all, but in the early scenes you can see the real candles.

The broomstick flying posed a bit more of a challenge. We brought in a kid from the local area, sat him on a broom in the workshop, put some foot pedals in and worked out what the most comfortable and best-looking riding position was. Suspended from a pole arm, with hydraulic gimbal heads enabling it to move in any direction, we worked out the young actors could sit on a bicycle seat mounted on the broom and have a totally fluid movement backwards and forwards, and up and down. In those early days Dan, Emma and Rupert came down to train and I explained it was just like riding a bike and all about first getting your balance. Whilst it was great fun, the kids didn't particularly enjoy being on the brooms for any great length of time, though I got them all padded bicycle shorts which helped a little.

Whilst the broom flying was mainly shot against green screens for CGI work to fill in the backgrounds, we did film some shots for real up at Alnwick Castle for the broomstick-flying lesson with Zoë Wanamaker as the teacher. There were little gimmicks such as a broom shooting up into their hands (via compressed air), and several shots were achieved by mounting a broom rig onto the back of a quad bike for some of the initial take-offs and landings. I was always a bit disappointed that we never got to do more but there were time limitations with the child actors all being so young, meaning our shooting days were limited and they could only be on set a certain number of hours before going to do their schoolwork and then home, so our shooting days never started before 8 a.m. and usually ended by 6 p.m. – which was wonderfully civilised for us crew members.

Having designed the broomstick rigs for the first film to suit 9–10-year-olds, we then had to redesign them film by film as the children were growing up fast and we needed stronger and more capable brooms for each new film – in fact, by the time we made the last film they weren't so much children as strapping young men and women. The whole size of everything changed throughout the ten years of making the movies, and we always strove to improve on the last film, particularly with more elaborate flying sequences, including moving from hydraulic actuation to electric actuators which were smoother, more controllable and less of a headache to put together, plus they

interfaced better with the CGI computers. Cooper was the first computer system we used by the way, before moving onto Flair later on.

The game of Quidditch – a fictional sport of wizards and witches consisting of two teams of seven players, each mounted on broomsticks, played on a hockey rink-sized pitch. Players would literally have to do all sorts of manoeuvres on a broom – sitting on it, hanging from it, tipping it end over end, spinning it round sideways etc. We designed specific broom rigs to do each of those specific movements either attached to pole arms or on specially made rigs. We frequently reconfigured these and used them several times over. Once all the separate movements were edited together, it looked incredibly exciting and showed just how agile wizards need to be.

We certainly had much more location work on the first film, as there was much more to set up in terms of the backstory of the Potter world including Hogwarts, the *Hogwarts Express*, the animals and so forth: it took us from Bamburgh Castle to Alnwick Castle and on to two of England's best Cathedrals – Durham and Gloucester – which was a huge privilege to be allowed to film in, let alone cover parts of them in snow and flood a corridor. It gave the film spectacle and a good sense of reality.

Hagrid (as played by Robbie Coltrane) was described as 'half-giant and half-human who is the gamekeeper and Keeper of Keys and Grounds of Hogwarts'. He had to tower over the child (and adult) actors, and to achieve that quickly and economically we used different perspective shots filmed in camera and we also had two different sizes of all the sets involved. Hagrid's hut was built in two different scales, one for shots with Martin Bayfield doubling Hagrid at 8ft tall, and then a three-quarter sized set into which Robbie Coltrane stepped; we filmed in one direction on one set and then the other way on the alternative set. It was trick photography with a lot filmed in camera, a technique that they also used in the *Lord of the Rings* films.

I must admit the first film was a bit of a learning curve for everyone, but that was a huge part of the fun – innovating, pushing boundaries, developing new technology and ideas whilst embracing old-school methods.

J.K. Rowling visited the studio a few times during the first film but if we ever had a meeting or situation when we were unsure about something or how someone looked, David Heyman would phone J.K. to ask the question and she always came back with an answer straightaway – she didn't have to think. She even sketched how she saw the layout of Hogwarts which was really useful to Stuart Craig our production designer.

Speaking of the sets, the magical, cobble-stoned shopping area of Diagon Alley was a false-perspective set – full-scale in the foreground and then reduced scale in the background to give a sense of size. It was actually pretty much rebuilt for every subsequent film, with a few added flourishes! A lot of the sets, including classrooms and teachers' rooms, were built, shot on and then revamped for the next film. The only sets that remained constant and unchanged throughout were the Great Hall and the Common Room.

Privet Drive – where Harry Potter lived in a cupboard under the stairs with the Dursleys at number 4 from the age of 1 – was actually a real cul-de-sac near Bracknell, and we shot on the outside of a real house with trained owls flying about and many CGI ones on the roof. Part way through filming there, it was decided to shoot the backstory of Hagrid arriving on a flying motorbike with the baby Harry to meet with Dumbledore and Professor McGonagall and leave young Harry on the Dursley doorstep. For reasons of cost and the complexity of installing a flying rig on the location, it was decided to build Privet Drive on the studio backlot; we devised and constructed a rig using two cranes, cables and a motorbike hanging on wires which we 'flew' in and out of the set, enabling us to shoot the entire scene at Leavesden. We also had an interior set of the Dursley house and it was there that we filmed the scene with all the letters arriving for Harry. I don't think that Chris Columbus thought we could achieve the sequence without the use of CGI but I managed to convince him to give it a try. We first got

hold of a letter-sorting machine similar to those used by the Post Office, but that didn't work the way we wanted, so we built twelve of our own 'letter firers' and had 25,000 envelopes printed, all addressed to HP. We then positioned the firers all around the set which gave the whole scene a great sense of reality. We ended up firing them through the letterbox, the fireplace and anywhere else that we could introduce them from. Mark Bullimore, who was part of my crew, also built a machine that was so accurate we could safely hit the actor Richard Griffiths right between the eyes with a 'soft' envelope.

Towards the end of the shoot, executive producer Mark Radcliffe came up to me outside one of the stage doors and said, 'We think we've just got the go-ahead for the next film, *Chamber of Secrets,* and we'd like you to work on it.' I was slightly taken aback – in a nice way – when Mark added, 'because we've never seen effects work first-time, like they do with you.' I shared that comment with all the boys on the effects team and that was my first inkling of a series taking off.

It was quite unique in the film business that we had the whole studio, backlot and buildings to ourselves which meant we didn't have to strike sets, store things elsewhere, and we could leave sets and rigs up and return if needed, offering a great scale of economy. An additional advantage of that is leaving sets standing means that you can theoretically go back to shoot pick-ups or additional shots and that was a rare benefit.

The Philosopher's Stone premiered and proved an unqualified success (taking almost $1 billion at the box office) which filled us all with pride and enthusiasm. Preparation on Harry Potter and the Chamber of Secrets (2002) had started almost as soon as we wrapped on the first film, and I must admit Chamber is my favourite film in the series and was the most enjoyable to work on, largely with the same key creative team behind it again, although David Barron came in as a new line producer to replace Duncan Henderson who returned to LA.

Along with flying broomsticks, there was a myriad of new and different things for us to get to grips with, including the Burrows (the Weasleys' house), Dumbledore's office (which houses the Sorting Hat, the Sword of Gryffindor and Dumbledore's desk), the Chamber of Secrets itself, plus Mr Weasley's flying car – created from a 1962 Ford Anglia 105E.

We had to find sixteen Ford Anglias in order to accomplish everything that was required, especially bearing in mind that films don't always shoot in continuity; they all had to match but look correct for all the different scenes in the film. There was a pristine car for when we first see it, a beaten-up one for after the incident with the Whomping Willow and a really dirty one for the escape from the Spider's Lair. They were also all rigged differently for these different scenes. For example, one was mounted on a gimbal – to simulate driving movement – and seated the kids; whilst another mounted on a pole arm was used to fly to Hogwarts; and another was attached to an American pickup truck with a pole arm mounted to a hydraulic head that rotated it, banked it, lifted it up and down, span it around, and the boot opened automatically. For its first appearance we literally flew it to the back window of Privet Drive, reversed in to get the trunk, then it spun round for Daniel Radcliffe to get in, before flying away. To control it I had a WALDO: a model of the real thing, consisting of a Dinky Car mounted on a model pole arm and whatever I did with the model, the real car matched perfectly. It worked really well but caused us a few headaches whilst perfecting it; the technology available nineteen years ago has improved so much over the intervening period. Of the other cars, three were adapted for stunt driving through the forest – two fitted with Cosworth engines and one with a V6. We also cut one car in half for shooting interior cutaways, whilst a further car was attached to a six-axis motion base which we dressed to look like the knuckle of the Whomping Willow. We then constructed two limbs of the Willow that could beat the car and appear to crush it; aluminium and lead panels built into that car allowed it to bend and buckle in places when hit by the limbs. We were able to film a lot of the damage to the car with the actors sitting inside which did add realism and we even had a large log thrust through the rear window. Everything was done as real as possible and was built with safety in mind – we were very aware that our actors were very young and at no time could we put them at risk of injury. Dan, Emma and Rupert were so receptive and accepted everything we asked of them – not always easy when you're standing in front of a piece of green screen with nothing to react to. They were brave when they needed to be – stuck up in the air on a broomstick, or when something blew up, or a car was being bashed – and I have to say full credit to the crew who treated and protected them like family and their wonderful parents for trusting us all. I think their only sadness was when they had to break off from the fantasy world to go for schooling.

The Chamber of Secrets was said to have been created under the dungeons of Hogwarts School during medieval times by Salazar Slytherin and was home to an ancient basilisk, which, according to legend, was intended to be used to purge the area of students born to Muggles (non-magical humans). The Chamber was described as being flanked with towering pillars that were entwined with carved wood, and an intricate 'snake door' lock. We built it to work for three weeks and would you believe, seventeen years later it's still working in the Harry Potter exhibit at the Warner Bros Studio Tour?

By the time *Chamber* was released, the books were becoming more and more successful, and Warner Bros were keen the films followed suit, but despite their huge popularity and financial success I'm still not sure why those early films received little recognition from the American Academy (the Oscars) as they were breaking boundaries. *Lord of the Rings* was a successful series and had been showered in Oscars, yet Potter didn't get a Visual Effects nomination until the third film (and then the last two films), but it still failed to be awarded a golden statuette. Admittedly we received eight BAFTA Visual Effects nominations (and won one) – one nomination for each film – so perhaps the UK voters recognise the craft of technicians on popular films.

After *Chamber*, Chris Columbus stayed on as a producer but stood down as director – and who can blame him as he'd worked so hard over three years and felt it was time to give someone else the chance to take the series forward.

Alfonso Cuarón, the Mexican director, was announced as the man set to helm *Harry Potter and the Prisoner of Azkaban* (2004). He was David Heyman's choice and on the surface, he seemed very much an outside bet to come in to this very British series. But he was an interesting and terrific director who wanted to put as much reality as possible into every scene, and having made a film with Warner Bros a few years earlier, they knew him well enough to realise he appreciated the difference in tone needed now that our hero was a teenager and darker powers and larger politics were at play in the storyline.

If you look carefully at *Azkaban*, you'll notice in the background of most shots there is something happening – nothing necessarily to do with the foreground, but something interesting or magic, and that was Alfonso's approach to the film along with making some of the sets a bit smaller with less light; Diagon Alley a bit shabbier and no big sweeping landscapes, only directly around Hogwarts.

The kids (as I affectionately refer to Dan, Emma and Rupert) had of course been used to working with Chris and so having him around, easing them into working with another director, was a great help.

Sadly, we had lost Richard Harris as Dumbledore as he died in August 2002. There was talk of both Ian McKellen and Peter O'Toole taking on the role, but ultimately it went to Michael Gambon. We had been blessed throughout with an amazing calibre of actors and could boast Maggie Smith, John Hurt, Julie Walters, Fiona Shaw, Leslie Phillips, John Cleese, Warwick Davis, Ralph Fiennes and Alan Rickman to name but a few. Alan, incidentally, walked around all day in character as Snape and was so convincing that when I had to set fire to his costume I remember thinking, with some trepidation, 'I've got to set fire to Snape' – not Alan.

My wife Rosie and I had been over from the USA for some time and were neglecting our home there. I wondered if these films were going to go on forever and if we should relocate back to the UK, but of course no one really knew, so I approached David Barron and said I'd love to do more, but I did want to spend a little time in the USA as Rosie was going back, and happily we came to an arrangement that every three weeks – providing there was nothing too complicated in the schedule – they would fly me back home for a week. I ended up with twelve or thirteen flights backwards and forwards, flying out on a Friday night and arriving back a week on Monday at 5 a.m. It was also helpful to remind people in Hollywood I was still around as I was conscious I might be looking for other work after this film – I never took my engagement for granted – and a bit of networking is always useful in that regard because whilst everyone knew I was doing Potter, they never bothered to phone to ask me to do anything else – apart from one occasion when Michael Apted asked me to help on a picture he was setting up, and I was able to put my American friends on it and visited a couple of times to check Michael was happy.

David Barron then left to do a film with Kenneth Branagh, and Callum McDougall came in as new line producer. I knew Callum from the Bond movies so it was a happy reunion.

In *Azkaban* we had a new vehicle, the Knight Bus – a triple-decker, purple AEC Regent III RT that assists stranded individuals of the wizarding community and operates at a very fast speed, where obstacles will jump out of its way. To make the bus we bought several double-decker buses and cut the top decks off and then attached two of these decks back onto one (single-decker) bus. We in fact made two of these triple-deckers, but for location work in central London they had to be broken down into sections – as they wouldn't go under any bridges! Every time we moved locations, we had to take them apart, put them on low loaders, move them and reverse the procedure – sometimes twice in a single night.

One of the buses was built on the chassis of a Volvo coach. It had a large, powerful engine and we added six tonnes of cod weight in the base so that it could be raced around corners without toppling over. Whenever you're on location, time is more limited than in a studio, and one of our locations couldn't have been in a busier area – right outside the Bank of England! – and we couldn't go in until after rush hour at 7 p.m. and had to be clear by 5 a.m. the next morning. It was there, on the five-point junction, Alfonso wanted the bus to spin around, so we bolted a rig down in the road, brought the bus in, lifted it on, connected up the hydraulics, added in passing cars, brought in the doubles and shot. I think we did it two or three nights in succession – very difficult logistics-wise.

One of the other major scenes in the movie I was heavily involved with was where Harry is on an ice lake from which he sees the Patronus Charm – a defensive spell which produces a silver, animal guardian, used to protect a witch or wizard against the evil Dementors who feed on happiness; but those very Dementors, in trying to stop Harry, made it so cold the lake froze over. As always, I thought it would be better to have a real ice lake rather than a wax one – I reasoned the actors would react to it better; it would be so cold you see their breath and it would be easier to repair any footprints or marks. We brought in a company that specialised in travelling skating rinks, built a shallow water tank on the huge H Stage at Shepperton Studios and put all the pipe work in, before filling it up and switching on the giant freezers. As luck would have it, it coincided with the hottest day in five years – the weather was never my friend on Potter movies. It was 90° on the stage and we were trying to freeze water, so extra coolers were installed and everything froze as planned. It was hard work for a few days, but the reality of the frozen lake did add to the scene.

Whilst I've spoken about making magic, I haven't yet mentioned magic wands.

We were using the wands made by the prop department and we fitted some small LED pea bulbs on the end to give off light as it conjures up spells and magic. LEDs were becoming more powerful so we constantly updated them, and then a request came in for a wand that featured an interactive light so as the wand moved about, it lit the actor. Someone suggested incorporating a quartz iodine bulb on the end, but we instead opted for a clump of LEDs placed in a clear Perspex ball, all facing outward. This gave a magical light effect and also made it much easier for CGI guys to enhance, as it was very precise.

Alfonso had brought a freshness to the movie, a new style and look whilst staying true to the formula already established – so he gave viewers everything they expected, but with a twist. He was a terrific director to work with and so receptive to ideas from all areas of the cast and crew. Having put everything he could into this movie, it was understandable he wanted to move on to other things, and as we moved towards the end of principal photography, word reached us that Mike Newell had been signed to direct the fourth Potter film – becoming the first British director to helm the series. Mike most famously directed *Four Weddings and a Funeral* (1994) and was again an interesting choice, particularly as he said he saw *Harry Potter and the Goblet of Fire* (2005) as 'a thriller'.

The story was largely based around competitive struggles – from the Quidditch World Cup to the Triwizard Tournament, which Harry is too young to enter yet his name is selected. The film's climax centred around Harry in one-on-one combat with his nemesis Voldemort (Ralph Fiennes), who murdered his parents thirteen years previously.

Mike pitched his thoughts to Dan as it being a paranoid thriller and told him specifically to watch *North by Northwest*, because he felt – as in Harry Potter's comfortable life – things suddenly started happening to the hero, pitching him up against the bad guy who seemingly had plans for him all along. In Harry's case, the bad guy was Voldemort and he brought with him a stressed, creepy feeling from the beginning of the film.

Mike started work on the film immediately we wrapped on *Azkaban,* and one of the first things that we addressed was the sequence in *Goblet* where the kids have to complete one of the challenges underwater. Everyone was concerned how we might film it all, and it was obvious we needed to figure this out very quickly. After trying some 'dry for wet' tests – where you film the actors on flying rigs with a little mist in the air and over-crank the camera to make everything seem slower – we agreed it didn't look very convincing. So we next built an underwater test tank, about 12ft deep and 20ft by 12ft. Although all the kids could swim, they'd never been underwater for any length of time or learned to dive. The idea was to give them a bit of experience in getting used to scuba equipment, along with taking their masks off to do a take and putting masks back on again – which was just as important. Those tests proved successful and looked good on film, so having been given the thumbs up, we discussed how big the water tank for the filming needed to be. I had a clear idea about this in my mind because I had worked in a few tanks

in my time, though the producers obviously thought I was stark raving mad when, to demonstrate, I chalked out the size of the proposed tank on the stage floor – it was virtually the full size of the stage. We knew that we'd have to dig out a very large hole to install a tank that was 18m by 18m wide and 6m deep. After a lot of planning and design it was approved and work commenced, but we then discovered that we'd have to take geological samples first as no one quite knew what was down there, including unexploded bombs from the Second World War!

To support the walls of the tank we needed to drive in steel piles but would you believe, we couldn't find a pile driver big enough to do the job, but small enough to fit under the stage roof! But where there's a will ... a chap called Mark Gent found a way.

Meanwhile, we started designing a water-purification, -filtration and -heating system for the ½ million gallons of water. We also had to design an underwater viewing chamber with 3in low-lead glass, so it didn't colour things green. This was double laminated and it meant the director and director of photography could sit and watch what was happening in the tank without getting their feet wet. Once completed, the tank took five days to fill with water and another five days to heat.

We put in a huge sand-filtration system with UV purification; this enabled us to reduce the level of chlorine in the water and more importantly, accurately control the pH levels which, if too high or too low could irritate the actors' eyes when they were in the water for long periods. Inside we built an underwater camera track that we could tow backwards and forwards, plus an underwater habitat near the bottom for the actors to go in and rest – it had a window and a constant supply of fresh air. This was important because the more you go up and down at that depth the more it reduces your allowable dive time. It also had a loudspeaker and microphone to save them constantly surfacing between set-ups. Between takes, they could duck in and chat with the director on the speaker system. We had dive doctors to check everyone and ensure that they were fit to dive and a strict 'no peeing in the water' policy. I actually think it was cleaner than Evian, especially as all ½ million gallons went through the filters every two hours.

We filmed on and off for three months and we also built two skimmers to keep the surface clean and remove any dust or rubbish that might blow into the tank. The stage doors had to be kept closed as much as possible to keep leaves and dust out, and we put in giant dehumidifiers because the water temperature was very warm and when the air temperature was cool, condensation would form and would run down the walls and soak everything in the stage. It all worked very well and the tank is still running today and used quite frequently at the studio.

Mike Newell was very good with the actors and in fact brought in the wonderful Miranda Richardson as Rita Skeeter, a scurrilous gossip reporter, whilst Brendan Gleeson came in to play 'Mad-Eye' Moody, an eccentric Hogwarts professor. Though Mike was the first to admit he'd never worked on a film with so many effects before, he seemed quite happy to use a lot of CGI, unlike Alfonso, who kept pushing for as much as possible to be done in camera.

When Harry faced a Hungarian Horntail dragon during the Triwizard Tournament we had great fun with giving it life and fire – apparently Hungarian Horntails can shoot fire as far as 50ft. With yellow eyes, black scales, bronze horns and spiky tails, they really are rather scary.

Goblet was the mid point in the series and I felt from there onwards, it tended to lean more and more into CGI, which was then becoming cheaper and being cheaper often scores above everything else. Not that I'm anti-CGI, but it's not always the best way of doing things, I feel.

Warner Bros appeared to be keen to keep the release pattern going which meant that as one film approached the end of shooting, the next had to be in preparation.

CHAPTER 14

BROOMSTICKS AND MAGIC: PART TWO

David Yates was approached to take over director duties on *Harry Potter and the Order of the Phoenix* (2007) and again brought a slightly different approach. He had a TV-heavy resume and brought his own style of film-making to the movie and like Mike Newell before him, he wasn't a director steeped in big effects films. He was keen to focus on bringing the child characters into the adult world, and it was to be the film that featured the first Potter kiss.

David did bring in a new second unit director, taking over from Peter MacDonald on the previous three films, and also replaced first assistant Chris Carreras who had worked so well on all four Potters to date. I was very sad to see them both leave, but it is very much the director's choice who he has in key positions.

There was certainly more CGI and less in-camera effects and I also noticed David liked to review every single shot the second unit and model unit did, to ensure his vision was carried through.

Order of the Phoenix proved a great success and David Yates was invited to stay on to direct the next, *Harry Potter and the Half-Blood Prince* (2009) which was an altogether warmer film. Whilst *Order of the Phoenix* dealt with teenage angst and a bit of a struggle against authority, this had a much richer and more romantic feel to it. Midway through production, we began to hear rumours that the last book in the series, *Harry Potter and the Deathly Hallows* might be split into two movies because producer David Heyman felt there was so much in that book, with so many rich characters, one movie alone couldn't do full justice to the book. It wasn't a purely commercial decision, as some trade press suggested, as it's actually a book of two halves and if they'd made it as one movie, they'd have to lose a lot or make a very long film. Of course, two films were an appealing consequence and also offered some economies of scale when shooting back-to-back.

By this time, we were filming mainly in the studio with green screen rather than on location and this required a lot more CGI for both the backgrounds and for the general effects. We however did shoot quite a lot of elements for the visual-effects team, for example, when Dumbledore and Voldemort have a wand battle in the Ministry of Magic, it called for 'He who shall not be named' to be trapped in a water bubble so we made large Perspex balls with water running over them or just swirling water round inside them. I also took a small unit out on the Leavesden runway to film a selection of fire elements with all sorts of furniture burning or exploding for them to cut, copy or replicate in CGI – it helped the digital-effects guys because they had real material to work with. We also had quite a lot to do for the destruction of Hogwarts! In fact, blowing it up was one of my favourite effects in all the movies; one part of it was done with a long tracking shot in the courtyard. I talked at great length to David Yates about it and how we could do it and include the actors and stuntmen.

We devised a set-up with seven cameras, some of them tracking, and we blew up as much as we could, making it look fiery and spectacular. As always with those shots, you have to be very precise, especially making sure the cameras, actors and crew were all where they should be. Timing and positioning is so important and not just to ensure safety but also to make sure that the explosions are in frame when they go off. It is quite complex to work out and does require multiple firing positions for the effects men on the switchboxes.

Those shots were then extended out with CGI.

The set was built out of a non-flammable foam and as per normal safety procedure, we had the film-industry fire-brigade company on standby which was just as well because a fire did develop but it was safely extinguished.

From beginning on *Philosopher's Stone* to ending on *Harry Potter and the Deathly Hallows: Part 2* in 2011, the films certainly became bigger and more expensive and that was reflected in the box office, proving the popularity of the series never diminished.

It was a sad day when we finished the last shot. We'd been a family for a decade and the kids had grown up with us. Fortunately, we still had a Quidditch flying sequence to film with the main actors for the Orlando Universal Studios so it wasn't quite bye-bye for me.

Once all the filming was finally completed and all the equipment stored or returned, we started to get involved with the plans to turn Leavesden into a permanent studio with a WB Studio Tour and a large Harry Potter exhibit. They planned to literally gut the Leavesden site and build brand-new stages, offices and workshops and make it a permanent base for Warner productions and devote two stages to the tour.

As I write this, the tour has been open for over seven years and there are more people visiting today than when it opened – and we've just added a huge extension to accommodate new sets. We keep adding things like Platform 9¾ with the train, the forest with big spiders, and more – it certainly keeps me busy!

After Potter, I did work on one more film, which was hugely, hugely enjoyable. It came about through the Mormon Church; I received an email from a colleague I'd worked with in LA who was a member of the church and said he had some friends coming to the UK making a film about the Bible and told them to call me. The church had its own film team, and they'd be largely shooting in Sicily when I met them. They spoke to me about how they might film Jesus walking on water and calming the tempest, so I flew to Rome and scouted Cinecittà Studios with them. But it didn't really work there so we decided to go to Pinewood and film on the outdoor tank. It really was a joyous experience to work with such lovely people.

I've had a few calls about other films, but it would have to be something I really wanted to do, with people I really wanted to work with to tempt me back. The way films are made nowadays is so different to the way we used to work for a number of reasons. I guess what I'm saying is I feel very lucky and very privileged to have had such amazing times and whilst it was hard work and long hours, for the most part we got everything done efficiently, on time, on budget and with a relatively small team – and that's the way I'd like to remember things.

Mike Turk, JR & Phil Hobbs: my two best men at our wedding

FINAL NOTE

I was asked recently what I would like to do if I could be 16 years old and start again. My reply was, 'I would like to do exactly what I have done for the last fifty-plus years ... ALL OVER AGAIN!'

APPENDIX

JOHN RICHARDSON FILMOGRAPHY

All dates given are for the year of production rather than the release date.

Working as Special Effects Assistant to Cliff Richardson			
Year	**Film**	**Director**	**Notes**
1960	Exodus	Otto Preminger	
1961	Lawrence of Arabia	David Lean	
1962	The Victors	Carl Foreman	
1963	The 7th Dawn	Lewis Gilbert	
	Lord Jim	Richard Brooks	
1964	Judith	Daniel Mann	
	Operation Crossbow	Michael Anderson	
1965	Help!	Richard Lester	
	Arabesque	Stanley Donen	
	A Funny Thing Happened on the Way to the Forum	Richard Lester	Unit Supervisor
	Dracula Prince of Darkness	Terence Fisher	
	Pope Joan	Michael Anderson	Work on fire scenes
1966	Casino Royale	John Huston et al.	Unit Supervisor
	Dirty Dozen	Robert Aldrich	
1967	The Mercenaries a.k.a. Dark of the Sun	Jack Cardiff	
	The Lost Continent	Les Norman and Michael Carreras	
1968	The Battle of Britain	Guy Hamilton	Unit Supervisor
	The Adventurers	Lewis Gilbert	Unit Supervisor
1969	The Private Life of Sherlock Holmes	Billy Wilder	Unit Supervisor

Films as Special Effects Supervisor			
1967	Duffy	Robert Parrish	
	Play Dirty	André De Toth	Preparation only
	Leo the Last	John Boorman	
1970	The Firechasers a.k.a. Cause for Alarm	Sidney Hayers	
	The Railway Children	Lionel Jeffries	
	Sunday Bloody Sunday	John Schlesinger	
	Something Like the Truth a.k.a. The Offence	Sidney Lumet	
	A Touch of Class	Mel Frank	
	Zeppelin	Etienne Perrier	
	The Devils	Ken Russell	
1971	Straw Dogs	Sam Peckinpah	
	Young Winston	Richard Attenborough	
1972	Scorpio	Michael Winner	
	The Day of the Jackal	Fred Zinneman	
	Night Watch	Brian Hutton	
	Phase IV	Saul Bass	
1973	The Little Prince	Stanley Donen	
	The Great Gatsby	Jack Clayton	
	Mahler	Ken Russell	
	Callan	Don Sharp	
1974	Juggernaut	Richard Lester	
	Barry Lyndon	Stanley Kubrick	
	The Triple Echo	Michael Apted	
	Tommy	Ken Russell	Preparation only
	Rosebud	Otto Preminger	
	Hennessy	Don Sharp	
	Rollerball	Norman Jewison	
	Royal Flash	Richard Lester	
1975	Lucky Lady	Stanley Donen	
	The Omen	Richard Donner	
1976	A Bridge too Far	Richard Attenborough	

1977	The People That Time Forgot	Kevin Connor	
	Superman	Richard Donner	
	Warlords from Atlantis a.k.a Warlords of the Deep	Kevin Connor	
1978	Escape to Athena	George Pan Cosmatos	
	Flash Gordon	Nicolas Roeg	Preparation only on abandoned version
	The Spaceman and King Arthur a.k.a. Unidentified Flying Oddball	Russ Mayberry	
1979	Moonraker	Lewis Gilbert	
	ffolkes a.k.a. North Sea Hijack	Andrew McLaglen	Special Effects & Model Unit Director
	The Watcher in the Woods	John Hough	
1980	Raise the Titanic	Jerry Jameson	Special Effects & Miniatures
	A Tale of Two Cities	Jim Goddard	
1980	Pirates	Roman Polanski	Preparation only
	Tai Pan	John Guillermin	Preparation only
1981	Five Days One Summer	Fred Zinneman	
	Ladyhawke	Richard Donner	Full production beginning in 1983
1982	Trail of the Pink Panther	Blake Edwards	
	Curse of the Pink Panther	Blake Edwards	
	Octopussy	John Glen	All Special & Visual Effects & Model Unit sequences
1983	Slayground	Terry Bedford	
1984	A View to a Kill	John Glen	All Special & Visual Effects & Model Unit sequences
1985	Aliens	James Cameron	
1986	The Living Daylights	John Glen	All Special & Visual Effects & Model Unit sequences
1987	Willow	Ron Howard	
1988	Licence to Kill	John Glen	All Special & Visual Effects & Model Unit sequences
1989	Treasure Island	Fraser Heston	
1990	Highlander II: The Quickening	Russel Mulcahy	

	Aces: Iron Egale III	John Glen	All Special & Visual Effects & Model Unit Director & Second Unit Director
1991	Far and Away	Ron Howard	Special Effects & Models
	Christopher Columbus: The Discovery	John Glen	Special Effects and Second Unit Director
1992	Cliffhanger	Renny Harlin	Special Effects on all Units and Models
	Ghost in the Machine	Rachel Talalay	
1993	Love Affair	Glenn Gordon Caron	Special Effects & VFX & Model Unit sequences
1994	Crusade (unproduced)	Paul Verhoeven	Preparation only
	Tenderfoots a.k.a. Bushwhacked	Greg Beeman	
1995	The American President	Rob Reiner	
	Broken Arrow	John Woo	
1996	Starship Troopers	Paul Verhoeven	
1997	Tomorrow Never Dies	Roger Spottiswoode	Model direction and underwater material
1998	Deep Blue Sea	Renny Harlin	
1999	The World is not Enough	Michael Apted	Model direction and underwater material
2000	The Family Man	Brett Ratner	
2001	Harry Potter and the Philosopher's Stone	Chris Columbus	
2002	Harry Potter and the Chamber of Secrets	Chris Columbus	
2002	Die Another Day	Lee Tamahori	Model direction
2003	Harry Potter and the Prisoner of Azkaban	Alfonso Cuarón	
2004	Harry Potter and the Goblet of Fire	Mike Newell	
2006	Harry Potter and the Order of the Phoenix	David Yates	
2007	Harry Potter and the Half Blood Prince	David Yates	
2008	Harry Potter and the Deathly Hallows: Part 1	David Yates	
2010	Harry Potter and the Deathly Hallows: Part 2	David Yates	
2011	The Story of Jesus (TV)		
2011 to 2019 Various films as Water Tank Supervisor and The Warner Bros Studio Tour			

OTTO PREMINGER PRESENTS
PAUL NEWMAN · EVA MARIE SAINT
RALPH RICHARDSON · PETER LAWFORD
LEE J. COBB · SAL MINEO · JOHN DEREK
HUGH GRIFFITH · GREGORY RATOFF
JILL HAWORTH IN "EXODUS"

MARIUS GORING · ALEXANDRA STEWART · MICHAEL WAGER · MARTIN BENSON · PAUL STEVENS · BETTY WALKER · MARTIN MILLER
VICTOR MADDERN · GEORGE MAHARIS · JOHN CRAWFORD · SAMUEL SEGAL · SCREENPLAY BY DALTON TRUMBO · BASED ON THE
NOVEL BY LEON URIS · MUSIC BY ERNEST GOLD · PHOTOGRAPHED IN SUPER PANAVISION 70. TECHNICOLOR® BY SAM LEAVITT · TODD
AO STEREOPHONIC SOUND · ART DIRECTOR RICHARD DAY · A U.A. RELEASE · PRODUCED AND DIRECTED BY OTTO PREMINGER

From the creators of "Th
Columbia Pictures presents The SA

LAWRENCH

❝I deem him one of the great
...we shall never see his like agai
It will live in the annals of war...It

ALEC GUINNESS · ANTHONY QUINN
JACK HAWKINS · JOSE FERRER
ANTHONY QUAYLE · CLAUDE RAINS · ARTHUR
PETER O'TOOLE as 'LAWRENCE' · OMAR SHARI
ROBERT BOLT · SAM SPIEGEL · DAVID LEAN · TECHNICOLOR

Adventure that reaches across the world!

JIM

RD BROOKS

ES CURT
ON·JURGENS

ACK PAUL
WKINS·LUKAS

T DALIAH
·LAVI "The
Girl"

D·Music by BRONISLAU KAPER

A Columbia Pictures Release·Keep Films Co-Production

N 70" TECHNICOLOR"

DRACULA
PRINCE OF DARKNESS

CHRISTOPHER LEE · BARBARA SHELLEY · ANDREW KEIR   FRANCIS MATTHEWS·SUZAN FARMER   WALTER BROWN   PHILIP LATHAM
CHARLES TINGWELL·THORLEY WALTERS

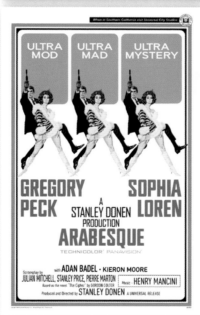

ULTRA   ULTRA   ULTRA
MOD   MAD   MYSTERY

GREGORY   SOPHIA
PECK   LOREN

A
STANLEY DONEN
PRODUCTION

ARABESQUE
TECHNICOLOR® PANAVISION®

with ADAN BADEL · KIERON MOORE

Screenplay by
JULIAN MITCHELL, STANLEY PRICE, PIERRE MARTON   Music   HENRY MANCINI

Based on the novel "The Cipher" by GORDON COTLER

Produced and Directed by STANLEY DONEN   A UNIVERSAL RELEASE

"HELP! I'm   "HELP! I'm   "HELP! I'm   "HELP!
kidnapped!" lost on a   surrounded   keep our
             tropic island!" by women!" city clean!"

STOP WORRYING!

HELP!

IS ON THE WAY!
The Colorful Adventures of

THE BEATLES
are more Colorful than ever...

LEO McKERN

ELEANOR BRON · VICTOR SPINETTI · ROY KINNEAR

EASTMANCOLOR   UNITED ARTISTS RELEASE

Something for Everyone!

ZERO MOSTEL • PHIL SILVERS

JACK GILFORD • BUSTER KEATON

In A MELVIN FRANK Production

**"A FUNNY THING
HAPPENED ON THE WAY
TO THE FORUM"**

CO-STARRING
MICHAEL
CRAWFORD
MICHAEL
HORDERN

Screenplay by MELVIN FRANK and MICHAEL PERTWEE Based upon the stage play produced by HAROLD S. PRINCE
Music and Lyrics by STEPHEN SONDHEIM Book by BURT SHEVELOVE & LARRY GELBART
Produced by MELVIN FRANK Directed by RICHARD LESTER
COLOR by DeLuxe | SUGGESTED FOR MATURE AUDIENCES. | Released thru **UNITED ARTISTS**

**CHARLES K.
FELDMAN**
presents
A FAMOUS ARTISTS PRODUCTIONS LTD.
CASINO ROYALE
Starring
**PETER SELLERS
URSULA ANDRESS
DAVID NIVEN
WOODY ALLEN
JOANNA PETTET
ORSON WELLES
DALIAH LAVI**
Guest Stars
**DEBORAH KERR
WILLIAM HOLDEN
CHARLES BOYER
JEAN PAUL
BELMONDO
GEORGE RAFT
JOHN HUSTON**
and Co-Starring
**TERENCE COOPER
BARBARA BOUCHET**
with
**GABRIELLA LICUDI
TRACY REED
TRACEY CRISP
KURT KASZNAR
ELAINE TAYLOR
ANGELA SCOULAR**

*plus a Bondwagon full
of the most beautiful and
talented girls you ever saw!*

Produced by CHARLES K. FELDMAN and JERRY BRESLER
Directed by JOHN HUSTON, KEN HUGHES,
ROBERT PARRISH, JOE McGRATH, VAL GUEST
Screenplay by WOLF MANKOWITZ,
JOHN LAW, MICHAEL SAYERS
Suggested by the Ian Fleming novel
Music by BURT BACHARACH
PANAVISION® TECHNICOLOR®
A COLUMBIA PICTURES RELEASE

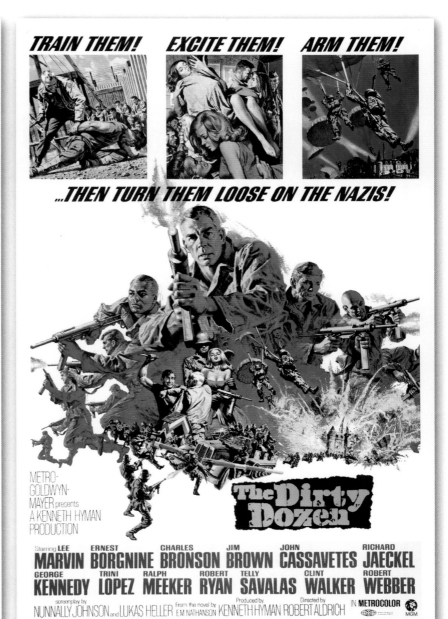

WHO SAYS PIRACY IS OBSOLETE ENTERTAINMENT?

COLUMBIA PICTURES Presents A MARTIN MANULIS Production

Duffy

Starring
JAMES COBURN · JAMES MASON
JAMES FOX and **SUSANNAH YORK**

Screenplay by DONALD CAMMELL and HARRYJOE BROWN JR.
Produced by MARTIN MANULIS · Directed by ROBERT PARRISH · TECHNICOLOR®

Hear Lou Rawls sing "I'm Satisfied" (The "Duffy" Theme) on Capitol Records

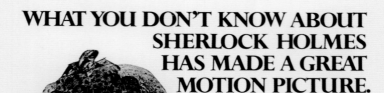

WHAT YOU DON'T KNOW ABOUT SHERLOCK HOLMES HAS MADE A GREAT MOTION PICTURE.

Everybody knows about the lightning-quick mind, the dazzling wit, the magnifying glass. But what about the little glass vials he so cunningly kept hidden.

And what about the security blunder that almost cost the British Empire its navy. And what about the woman who spent the night with him.

THE MIRISCH PRODUCTION COMPANY presents **BILLY WILDER'S**

THE PRIVATE LIFE OF SHERLOCK HOLMES
anything but elementary

starring
ROBERT STEPHENS · COLIN BLAKELY Produced and Directed by **BILLY WILDER** Written by **BILLY WILDER** and **I.A.L. DIAMOND**
Based upon the characters created by SIR ARTHUR CONAN DOYLE Music by MIKLOS ROZSA Filmed in PANAVISION® COLOR by DeLuxe®

United Artists
Entertainment from Transamerica Corporation

STYLE A   71/12

AFTER 20 YEARS,
WHAT DETECTIVE-
SERGEANT JOHNSON
HAS SEEN AND DONE
IS DESTROYING HIM.

**SEAN
CONNERY**
as Detective-Sergeant Johnson

**TREVOR
HOWARD**
in
"THE OFFENCE"

with
VIVIEN MERCHANT · IAN BANNEN
Written by JOHN HOPKINS · Produced by DENIS O'DELL · Directed by SIDNEY LUMET
United Artists

They had the perfect love affair.
Until they fell in love.

A Joseph E. Levine and Brut Productions Presentation

Starring
George Segal   Glenda Jackson

in A Melvin Frank Film A
Touch
Of Class

Co-starring
Paul Sorvino   Hildegard Neil

Music by **John Cameron** Songs by **George Barrie** and **Sammy Cahn**   Written by **Melvin Frank** and **Jack Rose**

Produced and Directed by **Melvin Frank**   An **Avco Embassy** Release   Technicolor® Panavision® | PG | PARENTAL GUIDANCE SUGGESTED

Some material may not be suitable for pre-teenagers

| Original Soundtrack available on **Brut Records** |

73/214

"TOUCH OF CLASS"

HELL HOLDS NO SURPRISES FOR THEM...

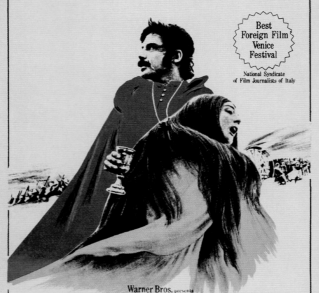

Best
Foreign Film
Venice
Festival

National Syndicate
of Film Journalists of Italy

Warner Bros. presents

VANESSA REDGRAVE / OLIVER REED

in KEN RUSSELL'S film of

THE DEVILS ®

A Robert H. Solo · Ken Russell Production
Screenplay by Ken Russell · Based on the play by John Whiting
and "The Devils of Loudun" by Aldous Huxley
Directed by Ken Russell · Panavision® · Technicolor®

 This programme is for "restricted" audiences and persons
under (18) years will NOT BE ADMITTED.
Proof of age may be required.

ABC PICTURES CORP. presents

DUSTIN HOFFMAN
in SAM PECKINPAH'S
"STRAW DOGS"

A DANIEL MELNICK Production

Starring SUSAN GEORGE as Amy   Music by JERRY FIELDING   Screenplay by DAVID ZELAG GOODMAN and SAM PECKINPAH

Produced by DANIEL MELNICK   Directed by SAM PECKINPAH

A SUBSIDIARY OF THE AMERICAN BROADCASTING COMPANIES, INC | COLOR | DISTRIBUTED BY CINERAMA RELEASING   **R**

RESTRICTED
Under 17 requires accompanying
Parent or Adult Guardian

72/10

When SCORPIO wants you...
there is no place to hide!

The most incredible manhunt of them all!

SCORPIO

THE MIRISCH CORPORATION presents

BURT LANCASTER · ALAIN DELON · PAUL SCOFIELD in A Michael Winner Film

"SCORPIO" co-starring JOHN COLICOS · GAYLE HUNNICUTT

Screenplay by DAVID W. RINTELS and GERALD WILSON
Story by DAVID W. RINTELS · Music by JERRY FIELDING

Produced by WALTER MIRISCH · Directed by MICHAEL WINNER · A SCIMITAR FILMS PRODUCTION

PG PARENTAL GUIDANCE SUGGESTED
SOME MATERIAL MAY NOT BE
SUITABLE FOR PRE-TEENAGERS

United Artists
Entertainment from
Transamerica Corporation

73/118

"SCORPIO"

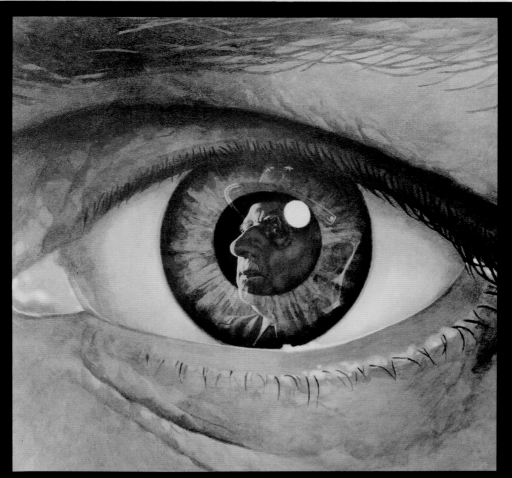

Fred Zinnemann's film of

THE DAY OF
THE JACKAL

A John Woolf Production
Based on the book by Frederick Forsyth

Edward Fox is The Jackal

Screenplay by Kenneth Ross Co-Producers: David Deutsch and Julien Derode
Directed by Fred Zinnemann Produced by John Woolf
Made by Warwick Film Productions and Universal Productions France S.A. Technicolor®
Distributed by Cinema International Corporation

PRINTED IN ENGLAND BY W. E. BERRY LTD BRADFORD

THE DAY THE EARTH WAS TURNED INTO A CEMETERY!

RAVENOUS INVADERS CONTROLLED BY A TERROR OUT IN SPACE... COMMANDED TO ANNIHILATE THE WORLD!

PHASE IV

When you can't scream anymore!

PARAMOUNT PICTURES PRESENTS "PHASE IV" Starring NIGEL DAVENPORT
MICHAEL MURPHY LYNNE FREDERICK Written by MAYO SIMON
Produced by PAUL B. RADIN Directed by SAUL BASS AN ALCED PRODUCTION
TECHNICOLOR® A PARAMOUNT PICTURE

PG PARENTAL GUIDANCE SUGGESTED
SOME MATERIAL MAY NOT BE
SUITABLE FOR PRE-TEENAGERS

74/51

"PHASE IV"

The entertainment
that loves a lot,
and lives a lot,
and gives
and gives
and gives
a lot.

Paramount Pictures Presents
A STANLEY DONEN FILM OF
LERNER AND LOEWE'S

THE LITTLE PRINCE

Richard Kiley Bob Fosse as the Snake Steven Warner and Gene Wilder as the Fox
Produced and Directed by STANLEY DONEN Associate Producer – A. Joseph Tandet
Screenplay and Lyrics by ALAN JAY LERNER Music by FREDERICK LOEWE

Based on the story
"THE LITTLE PRINCE" by Antoine deSaint-Exupéry
Technicolor®

G GENERAL AUDIENCES
All Ages Admitted

SOUNDTRACK ALBUM AVAILABLE ON ABC RECORDS

gone is
the romance
that was
so divine.*

Paramount Pictures presents
DAVID MERRICK'S PRODUCTION OF
A JACK CLAYTON FILM
ROBERT REDFORD and MIA FARROW

THE
GREAT
GATSBY

co-starring KAREN BLACK SCOTT WILSON SAM WATERSTON
LOIS CHILES and BRUCE DERN as Tom Produced by DAVID MERRICK
Directed by JACK CLAYTON Screenplay by FRANCIS FORD COPPOLA Based on the novel by
F. SCOTT FITZGERALD Associate Producer HANK MOONJEAN
Music Supervised and Conducted by Nelson Riddle In Color Prints by Movielab A Paramount Picture
*Copyright © 1924 by Irving Berlin. Copyright Renewed 1951 ORIGINAL SOUNDTRACK AVAILABLE ON PARAMOUNT RECORDS AND GRT TAPES.

74/89

"THE GREAT GATSBY"

YOU WILL PAY ME 1½ MIL...
THE WORLD'S GREATEST L...
LIKE A CAN OF SARDINES...
AND CHILDREN WILL DIE.

BR

Only one man to   His ship is at the   He feels the full   He
save 1200 lives!   mercy of Juggernaut!   fury of Juggernaut!   find

"JUGG

SEA ADV
HA

DAVID V. PICKER presents RICHARD HARRIS
A RICHARD LESTER Film with DAVID HEMMINGS · A
IAN HOLM · CLIFTON JAMES · ROY KINNEAR · Exec
Written and Produced by RICHARD DeKOKER · Directed by RIC

PG

ON DOLLARS BY DAWN OR

URY LINER WILL RIP OPEN

ND 1200 MEN, WOMEN,

GOOD DAY. —JUGGERNAUT

The Captain's woman: she too must submit!	For the first time he faces the truth!	Just one last chance to become a hero!

GREATEST
URE IN HISTORY
ST BEGUN!

MAR SHARIF in "JUGGERNAUT"

HONY HOPKINS · SHIRLEY KNIGHT

roducer DAVID V. PICKER · Associate Producer DENIS O'DELL

D LESTER

United Artists

JUGGERNAUT 74/273

Rosebud

An Otto Preminger Film

PETER O'TOOLE / RICHARD ATTENBOROUGH
CLIFF GORMAN / CLAUDE DAUPHIN / JOHN V. LINDSAY
PETER LAWFORD / and RAF VALLONE as GEORGE NIKOLAOS

co-starring ADRIENNE CORRI / AMIDOU / YOSEF SHILOA / BRIGITTE ARIEL
ISABELLE HUPPERT / LALLA WARD / KIM CATTRALL / DEBRA BERGER
Directed and Produced by Otto Preminger / Screenplay by Erik Lee Preminger
Based on the novel by Joan Hemingway and Paul Bonnecarrere

PG PARENTAL GUIDANCE SUGGESTED   COLOR by DeLuxe® / Filmed in Panavision®

United Artists
Entertainment from
Transamerica Corporation

STYLE C   75/86

"ROSEBUD"

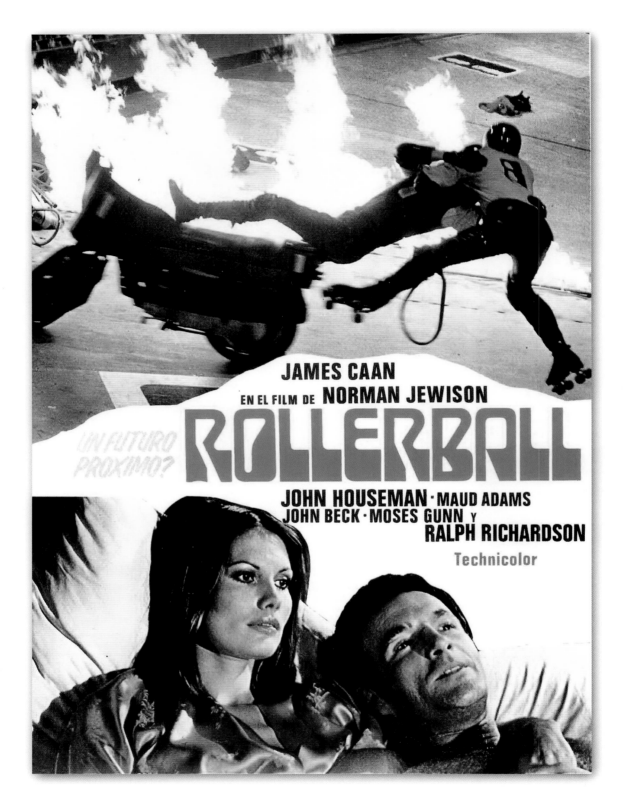

JAMES CAAN
EN EL FILM DE NORMAN JEWISON
ROLLERBALL

UN FUTURO
PROXIMO?

JOHN HOUSEMAN · MAUD ADAMS
JOHN BECK · MOSES GUNN Y
RALPH RICHARDSON

Technicolor

YOU HAVE BEEN WARNED

IF SOMETHING
FRIGHTENING
HAPPENS TO YOU
TODAY,
THINK ABOUT IT

IT MAY BE

THE OMEN

TWENTIETH CENTURY-FOX Presents

GREGORY PECK LEE REMICK
THE OMEN

A HARVEY BERNHARD-MACE NEUFELD PRODUCTION

Co-starring DAVID WARNER BILLIE WHITELAW

Executive Producer MACE NEUFELD Produced by HARVEY BERNHARD Directed by RICHARD DONNER

R RESTRICTED Written by DAVID SELTZER Music JERRY GOLDSMITH PANAVISION® Prints by DELUXE®

ORIGINAL SOUNDTRACK ALBUM ON TATTOO RECORDS AND TAPES. DISTRIBUTED BY R.C.A. RECORDS.

THE OMEN

FIRST 'THE LAND THAT TIME FORGOT'
THEN 'AT THE EARTH'S CORE'
NOW A FANTASTIC INCREDIBLE WORLD OF SAVAGE MYSTERY...

EDGAR RICE BURROUGHS'
The PEOPLE That TIME FORGOT

U

Samuel Z. Arkoff Presents A Max J. Rosenberg Production Starring **PATRICK WAYNE** in "THE PEOPLE THAT TIME FORGOT," An American International Picture
Co-Starring SARAH DOUGLAS · THORLEY WALTERS · DANA GILLESPIE · SHANE RIMMER And Guest Star **DOUG McCLURE**
Executive Producer Samuel Z. Arkoff · Screenplay by Patrick Tilley · Based on "THE PEOPLE THAT TIME FORGOT" by EDGAR RICE BURROUGHS
Music by John Scott · Produced by John Dark · Directed by Kevin Connor · Production Services by Cardinal Productions · Colour by Movielab   Released by Brent Walker Film Distributors Ltd.

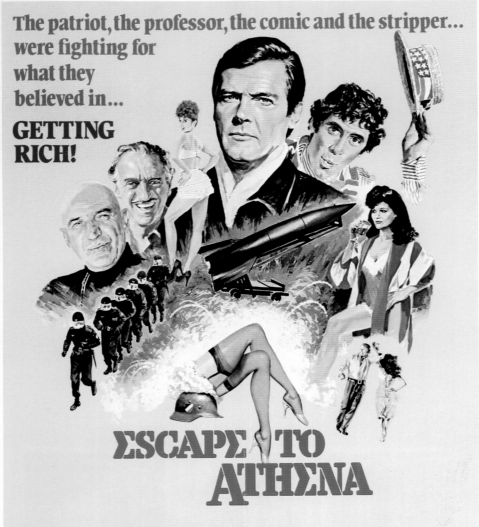

The patriot, the professor, the comic and the stripper...
were fighting for
what they
believed in...
**GETTING
RICH!**

**ΣSCAPΣ TO
ATHΣNA**

SIR LEW GRADE PRESENTS
A DAVID NIVEN, JR. /JACK WIENER Production
"ESCAPE TO ATHENA" A Film by GEORGE P. COSMATOS
ROGER MOORE   TELLY SAVALAS   DAVID NIVEN
STEFANIE POWERS   CLAUDIA CARDINALE
RICHARD ROUNDTREE   SONNY BONO and ELLIOTT GOULD
as Charlie
Music by LALO SHIFRIN Story by RICHARD S. LOCHTE and GEORGE P. COSMATOS
Screenplay by EDWARD ANHALT and RICHARD S. LOCHTE
Produced by DAVID NIVEN, JR. and JACK WIENER Directed by GEORGE P. COSMATOS

PANAVISION®   Associated Film from ENTERTAINMENT PG PARENTAL GUIDANCE SUGGESTED
Distribution   SOME MATERIAL MAY NOT BE SUITABLE FOR PRE-TEENAGERS
© 1979

790103

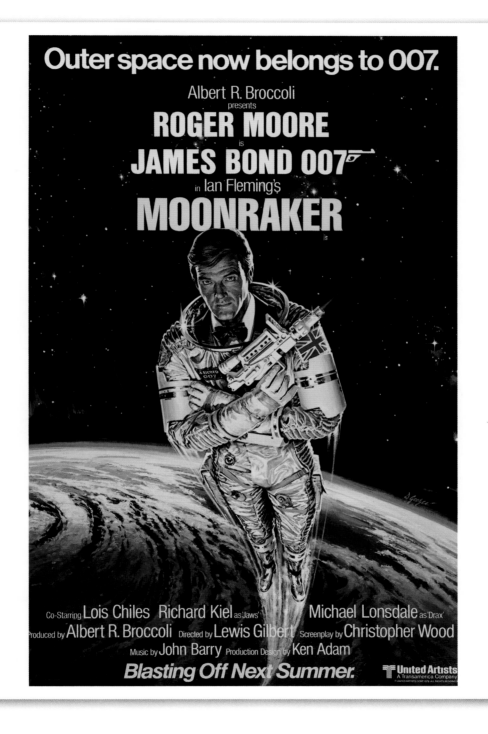

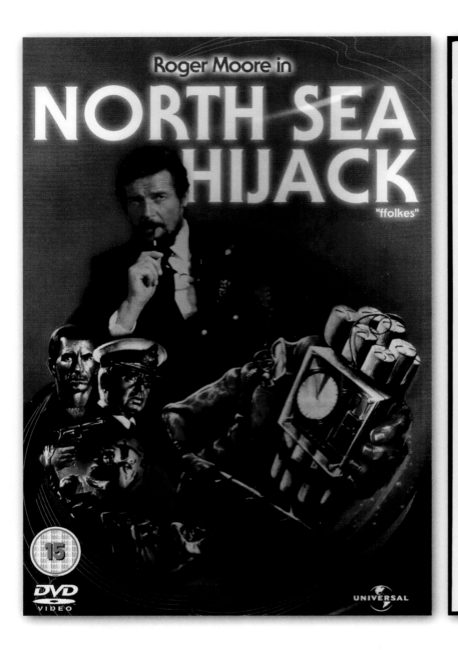

Roger Moore in

NORTH SEA HIJACK

"ffolkes"

15

DVD
VIDEO

UNIVERSAL

Once the
God himself cou

Then the
no man on earth c

Now—you wi
when v

RAISE
TITA

LORD GRADE
A MARTIN STARGER
"RAISE THE T
STARRING JASON ROBARDS · RICHARD JORDAN · DAV
Executive Producer MARTIN STARGER Produced By
Screenplay By ADAM KENNEDY Adaptation By ERIC HUGHES Bas
READ THE BANTAM BOOK
PG PARENTAL GUIDANCE
SOME MATERIAL MAY NOT BE S

UN FILM DE

FRED ZINNEMANN

CINQ JOURS
CE PRINTEMPS-LA

AVEC

SEAN CONNERY

ET, POUR LA PREMIÈRE FOIS A L'ÉCRAN

BETSY BRANTLEY ET LAMBERT WILSON

Un Film de FRED ZINNEMANN · SEAN CONNERY dans "CINQ JOURS CE PRINTEMPS-LA"

BETSY BRANTLEY · LAMBERT WILSON avec GÉRARD BUHR · ISABEL DEAN · JENNIFER HILARY · ANNA MASSEY · SHEILA REID

Produit et Réalisé par FRED ZINNEMANN

The newest and funniest 'Panther' of them all.

PETER SELLERS in BLAKE EDWARDS'

Trail of the Pink Panther

STARRING DAVID NIVEN ◆ HERBERT LOM ◆ RICHARD MULLIGAN ◆ JOANNA LUMLEY ◆ CAPUCINE
ROBERT LOGGIA ◆ HARVEY KORMAN ◆ BURT KWOUK ◆ MUSIC BY HENRY MANCINI ◆ STORY BY
BLAKE EDWARDS ◆ SCREENPLAY BY FRANK WALDMAN ◆ TOM WALDMAN ◆ BLAKE EDWARDS
GEOFFREY EDWARDS ◆ PRODUCED BY BLAKE EDWARDS AND TONY ADAMS
DIRECTED BY BLAKE EDWARDS

SOUNDTRACK AVAILABLE ON EMI / LIBERTY RECORDS & TAPES.

United Artists MGM/UA

PG PARENTAL GUIDANCE SUGGESTED

820140
TRAIL OF THE PINK PANTHER

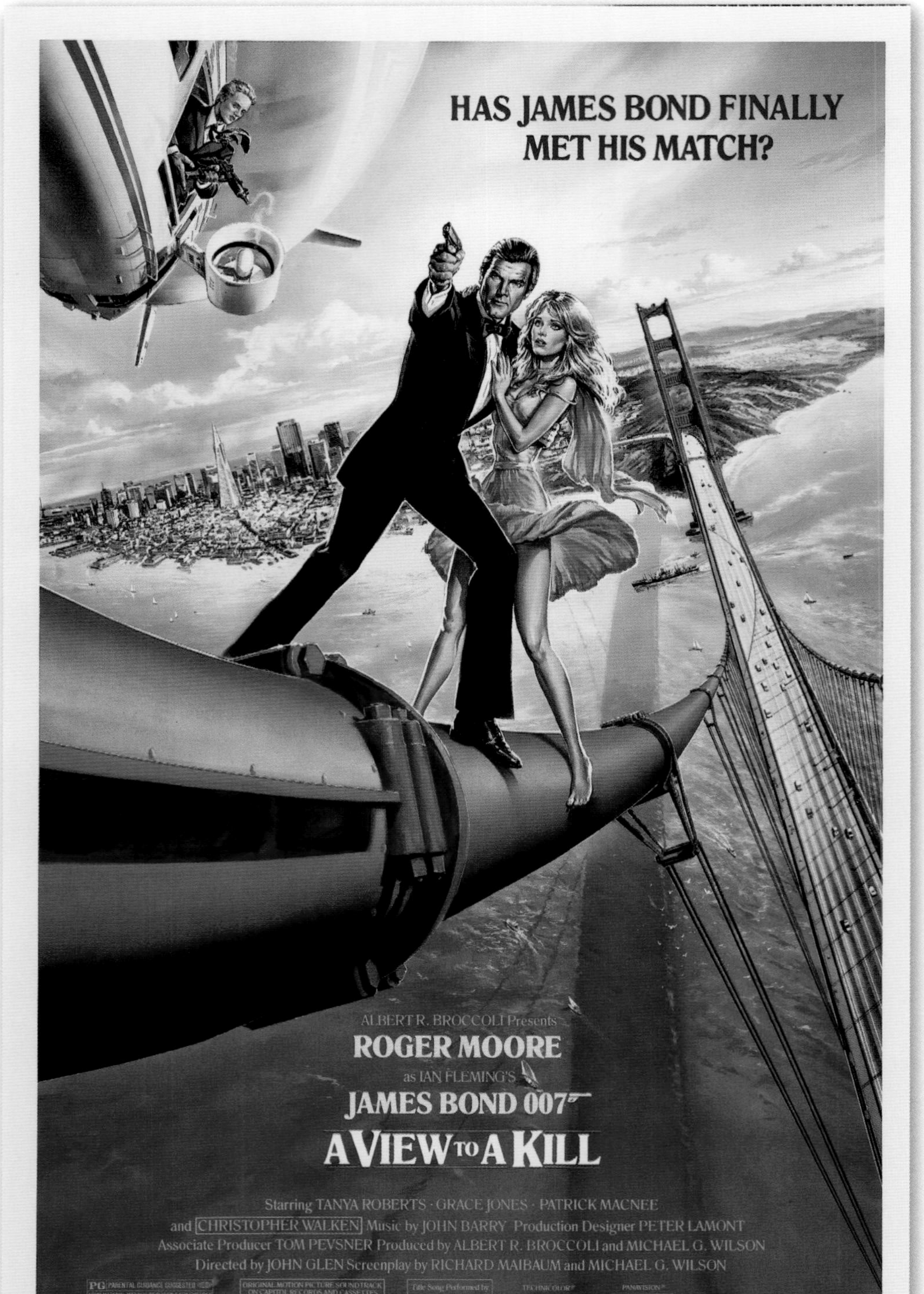
HAS JAMES BOND FINALLY
MET HIS MATCH?
ALBERT R. BROCCOLI Presents
ROGER MOORE
as IAN FLEMING'S
JAMES BOND 007
A VIEW TO A KILL
Starring TANYA ROBERTS · GRACE JONES · PATRICK MACNEE
and CHRISTOPHER WALKEN Music by JOHN BARRY Production Designer PETER LAMONT
Associate Producer TOM PEVSNER Produced by ALBERT R. BROCCOLI and MICHAEL G. WILSON
Directed by JOHN GLEN Screenplay by RICHARD MAIBAUM and MICHAEL G. WILSON
PG PARENTAL GUIDANCE SUGGESTED
ORIGINAL MOTION PICTURE SOUNDTRACK ON CAPITOL RECORDS AND CASSETTES
Title Song Performed by DURAN DURAN
TECHNICOLOR® Prints in METROCOLOR®
PANAVISION®
DOLBY STEREO

NS 850004B

THE NEW JAMES BOND . . . LIVING ON THE EDGE

ALBERT R. BROCCOLI

presents

TIMOTHY DALTON

as IAN FLEMING'S

JAMES BOND 007

THE LIVING DAYLIGHTS

STARRING MARYAM d'ABO · JOE DON BAKER · ART MALIK and JEROEN KRABBÉ

PRODUCTION DESIGNER PETER LAMONT MUSIC BY JOHN BARRY ASSOCIATE PRODUCERS TOM PEVSNER and BARBARA BROCCOLI

PRODUCED BY ALBERT R. BROCCOLI and MICHAEL G. WILSON DIRECTED BY JOHN GLEN SCREENPLAY BY RICHARD MAIBAUM and MICHAEL G. WILSON

TECHNICOLOR® PANAVISION® | ORIGINAL SOUNDTRACK ALBUM AVAILABLE ON W.E.A. RECORDS CASSETTES AND COMPACT DISCS | The Pretenders | a-ha |

THEIR MISSION UNOFFICIAL.
THEIR TACTICS UNCONVENTIONAL.
THEIR COURAGE UNBELIEVABLE.
ACES
IRON EAGLE III
THE HEIGHT OF ADVENTURE.

TOM CRUISE

He left behind everything he knew
for the only thing he ever wanted.

NICOLE KIDMAN

A RON HOWARD FILM

FAR AND AWAY

IMAGINE FILMS ENTERTAINMENT PRESENTS A BRIAN GRAZER PRODUCTION "FAR AND AWAY"
MUSIC BY JOHN WILLIAMS COSTUMES DESIGNED BY JOANNA JOHNSTON CO-PRODUCERS LARRY DeWAAY BOB DOLMAN FILM EDITORS MICHAEL HILL
DANIEL HANLEY PRODUCTION DESIGNED BY JACK T. COLLIS ALLAN CAMERON DIRECTOR OF PHOTOGRAPHY MIKAEL SALOMON, A.S.C.
EXECUTIVE PRODUCER TODD HALLOWELL STORY BY BOB DOLMAN & RON HOWARD SCREENPLAY BY BOB DOLMAN PRODUCED BY BRIAN GRAZER AND RON HOWARD
DIRECTED BY RON HOWARD A UNIVERSAL RELEASE

FILMED FOR THE FIRST TIME IN PANAVISION SUPER 70MM

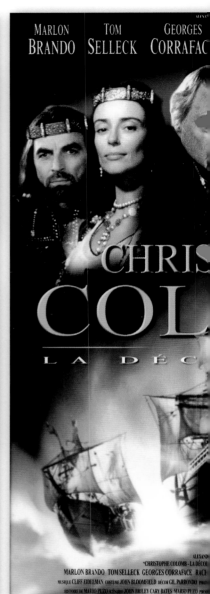

MARLON   TOM   GEORGES
BRANDO   SELLECK   CORRAFAC

CHRIS
COL
LA DÉC

"CHRISTOPHE COLOMB - LA DÉCOU
MARLON BRANDO TOM SELLECK GEORGES CORRAFACE RACI
MUSIQUE CLIFF EIDELMAN COSTUMES JOHN BLOOMFIELD DÉCOR GIL PARRONDO
HISTOIRE DE MARIO PUZO SCÉNARIO JOHN BRILEY CARY BATES MARIO PUZO PRO

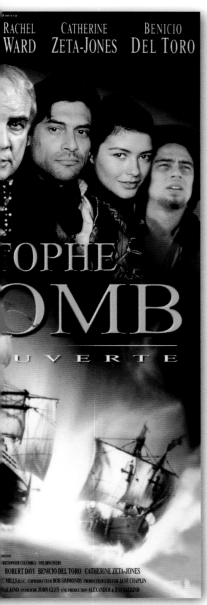

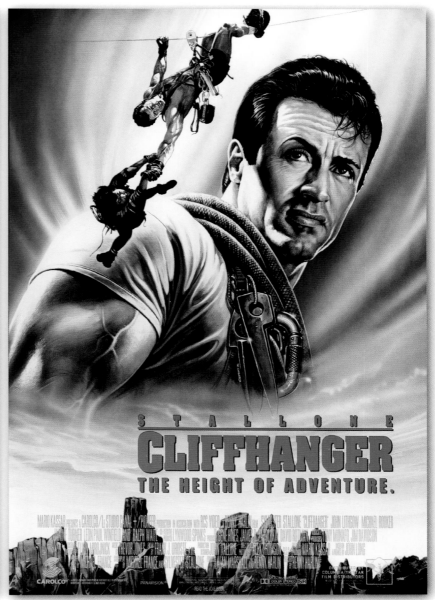

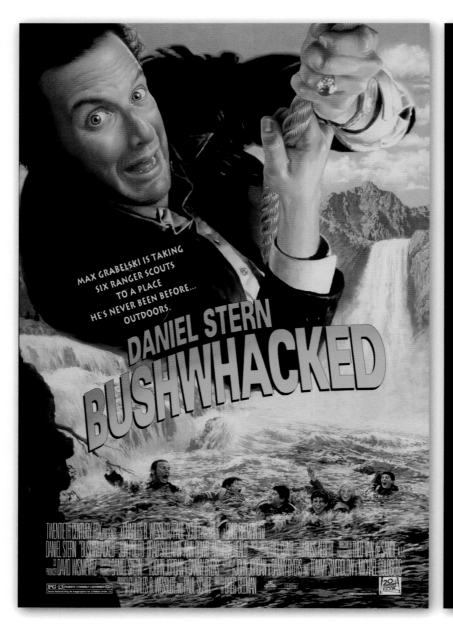

MAX GRABELSKI IS TAKING
SIX RANGER SCOUTS
TO A PLACE
HE'S NEVER BEEN BEFORE...
OUTDOORS.

DANIEL STERN
BUSHWHACKED

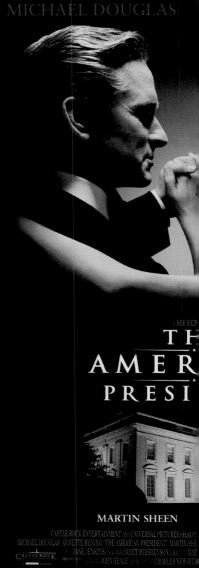

MICHAEL DOUGLAS

A ROB REIN

TH
AMERI
PRESI

MARTIN SHEEN

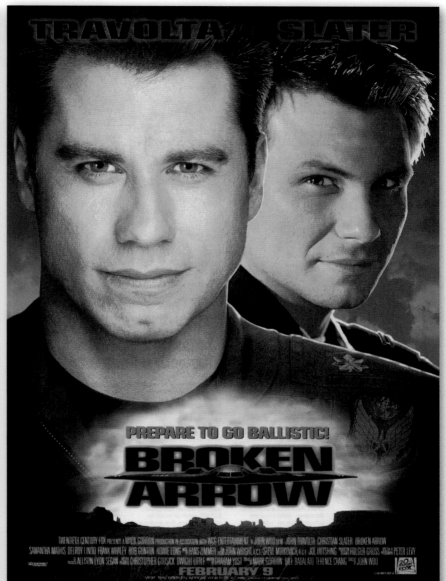

PREPARE TO GO BALLISTIC!

BROKEN
ARROW

BIGGER. SMARTER. FASTER. MEANER.

DEEP BLUE SEA

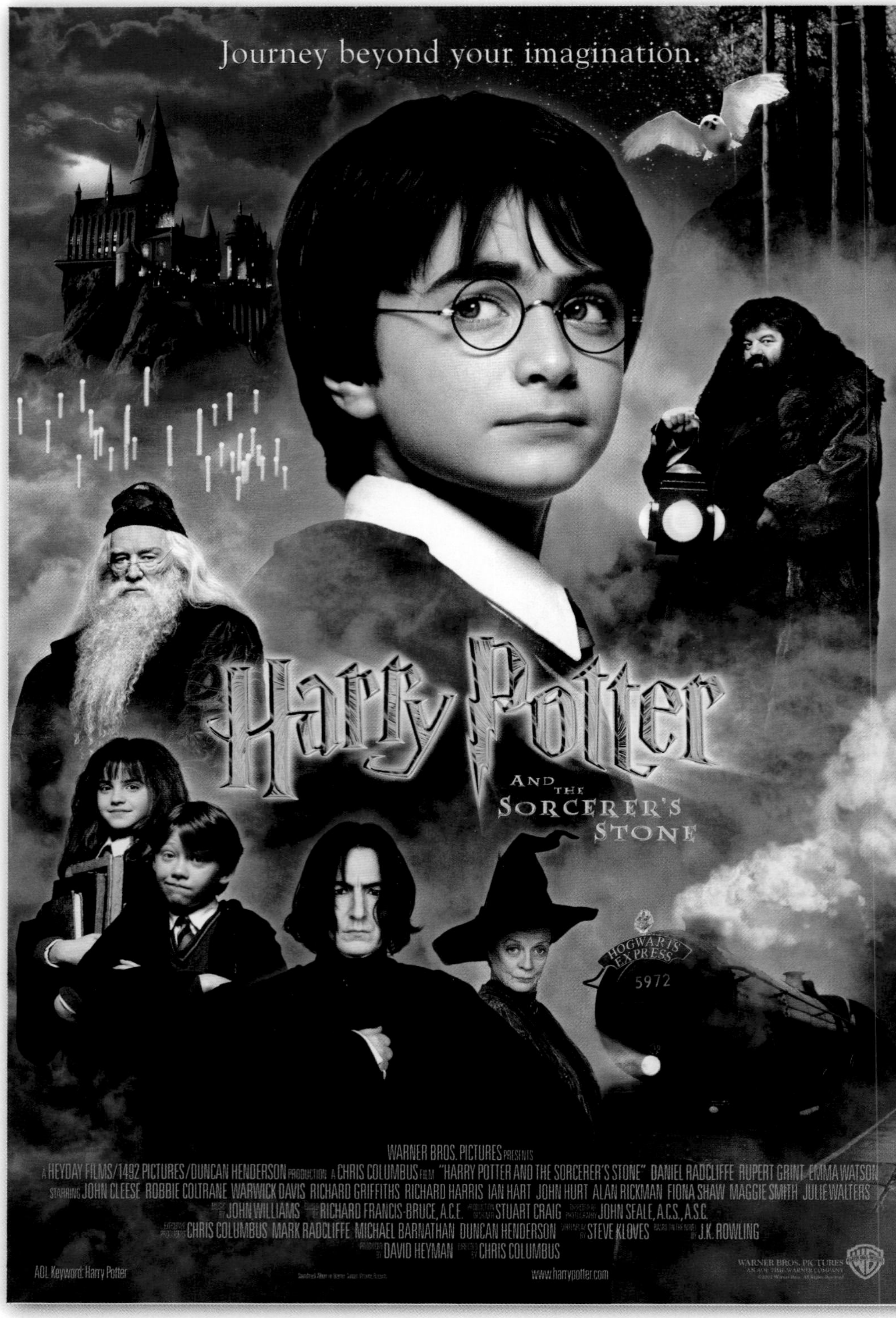

Journey beyond your imagination.
Harry Potter
AND THE SORCERER'S STONE
HOGWARTS EXPRESS
5972
WARNER BROS. PICTURES PRESENTS
A HEYDAY FILMS/1492 PICTURES/DUNCAN HENDERSON PRODUCTION A CHRIS COLUMBUS FILM "HARRY POTTER AND THE SORCERER'S STONE" DANIEL RADCLIFFE RUPERT GRINT EMMA WATSON
STARRING JOHN CLEESE ROBBIE COLTRANE WARWICK DAVIS RICHARD GRIFFITHS RICHARD HARRIS IAN HART JOHN HURT ALAN RICKMAN FIONA SHAW MAGGIE SMITH JULIE WALTERS
JOHN WILLIAMS RICHARD FRANCIS-BRUCE, A.C.E. STUART CRAIG JOHN SEALE, A.C.S., A.S.C.
CHRIS COLUMBUS MARK RADCLIFFE MICHAEL BARNATHAN DUNCAN HENDERSON STEVE KLOVES J.K. ROWLING
DAVID HEYMAN CHRIS COLUMBUS
AOL Keyword: Harry Potter
www.harrypotter.com
WARNER BROS. PICTURES

SOMETHING EVIL HAS RETURNED TO HOGWARTS!
Harry Potter
AND THE CHAMBER OF SECRETS
WARNER BROS. PICTURES PRESENTS
A HEYDAY FILMS/1492 PICTURES PRODUCTION A CHRIS COLUMBUS FILM "HARRY POTTER AND THE CHAMBER OF SECRETS"
DANIEL RADCLIFFE RUPERT GRINT EMMA WATSON STARRING KENNETH BRANAGH JOHN CLEESE ROBBIE COLTRANE
WARWICK DAVIS RICHARD GRIFFITHS RICHARD HARRIS JASON ISAACS ALAN RICKMAN FIONA SHAW
MAGGIE SMITH JULIE WALTERS JOHN WILLIAMS WILLIAM ROSS PETER HONESS, A.C.E. STUART CRAIG
ROGER PRATT, B.S.C. CHRIS COLUMBUS MARK RADCLIFFE MICHAEL BARNATHAN DAVID BARRON
STEVE KLOVES J.K. ROWLING DAVID HEYMAN CHRIS COLUMBUS
AOL Keyword: Harry Potter www.harrypotter.com

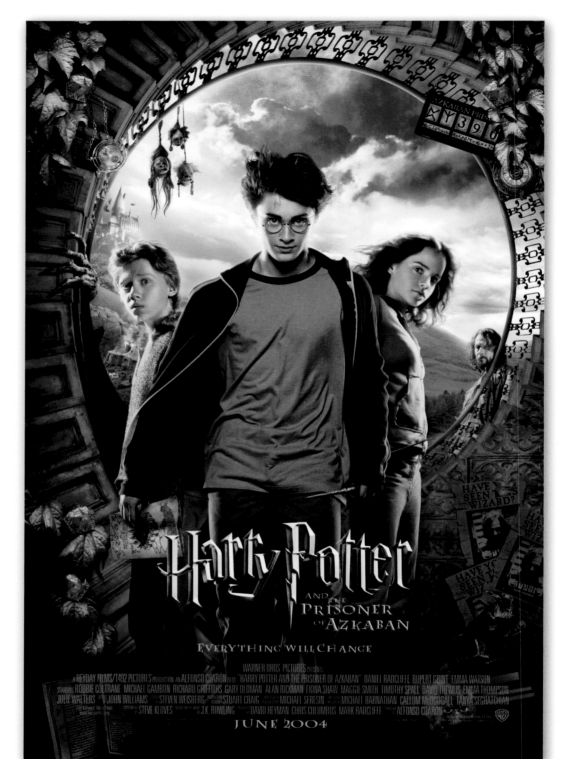

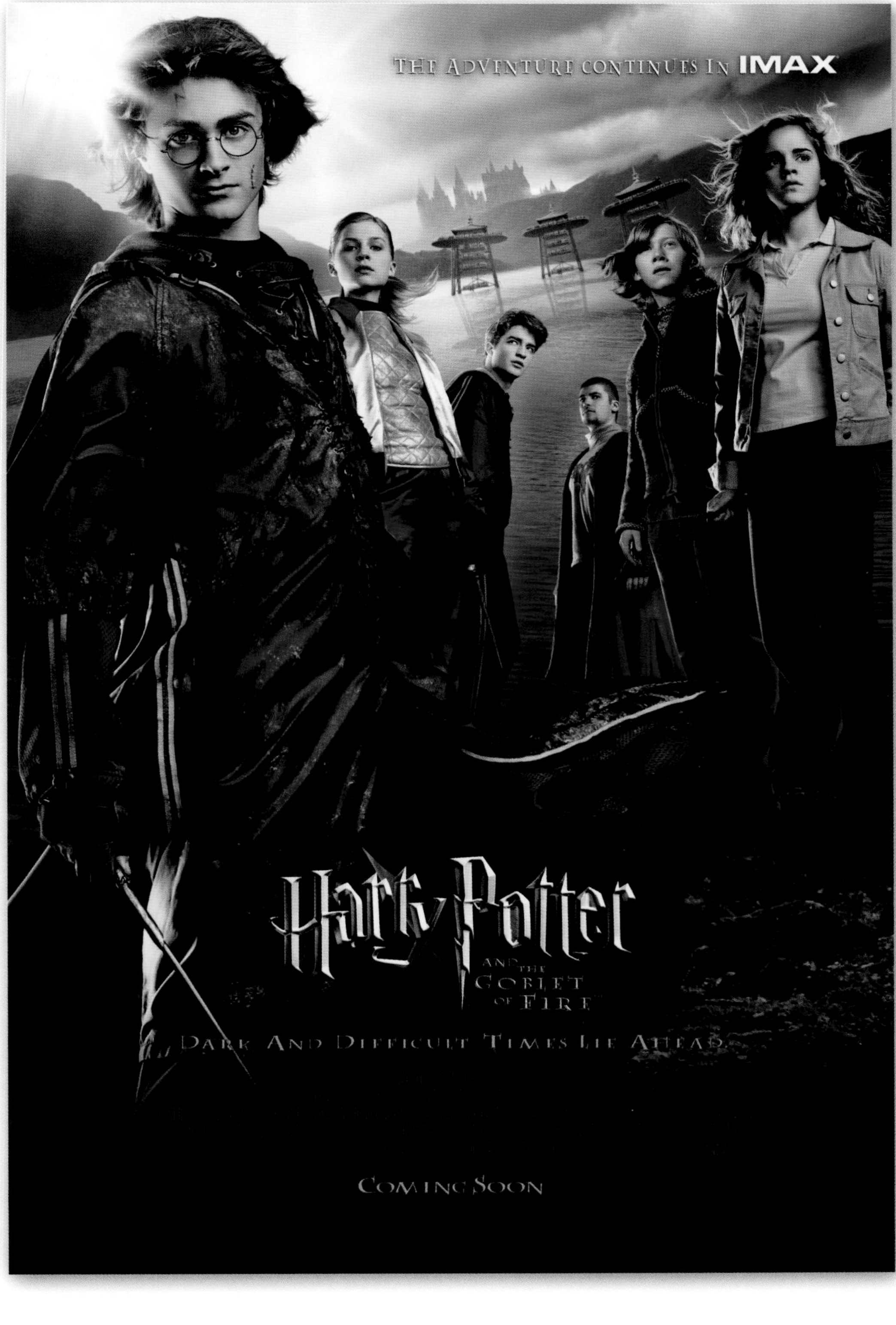
THE ADVENTURE CONTINUES IN IMAX
Harry Potter
AND THE GOBLET OF FIRE
DARK AND DIFFICULT TIMES LIE AHEAD
COMING SOON

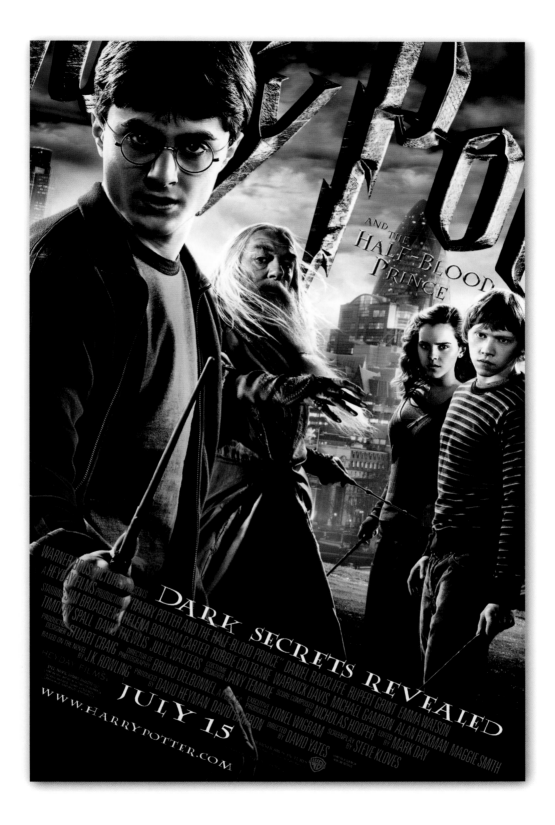

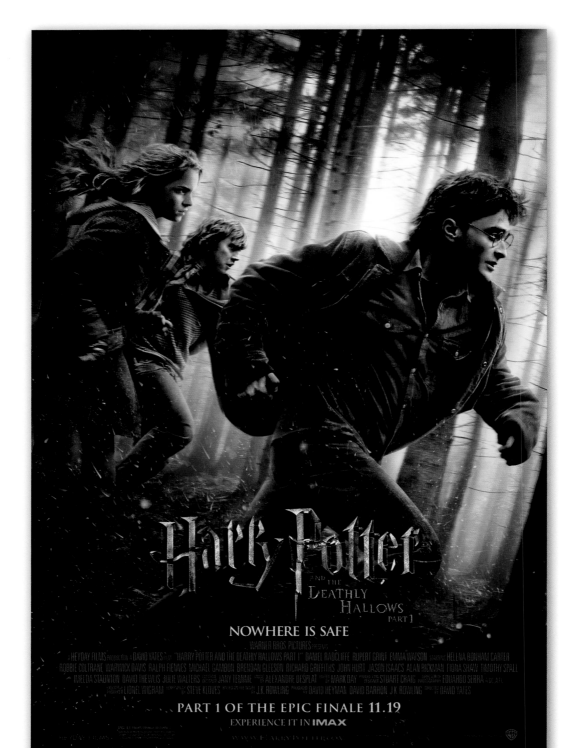

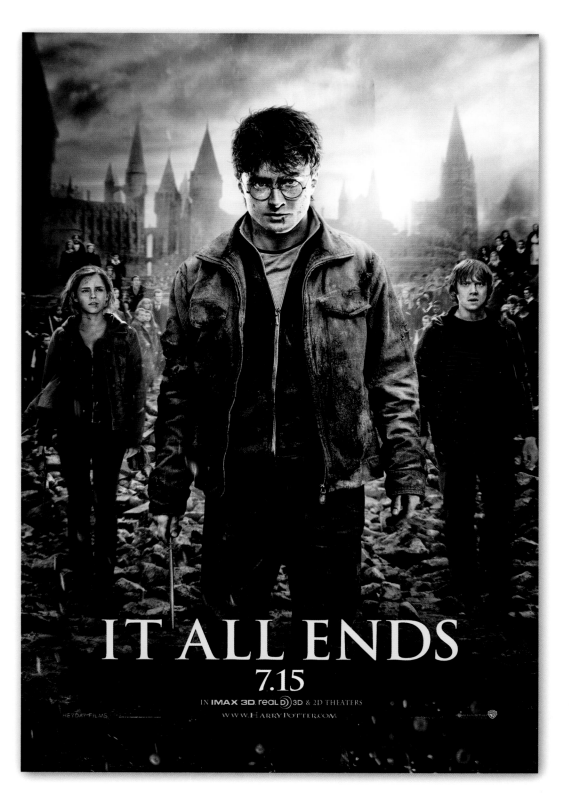

ACKNOWLEDGEMENTS

A huge thank you to Gareth Owen for his tremendous help in writing this book and a very special thank you to Rosie for being my inspiration and my guiding light.

Thanks also to: Iris Harwood and Robin Harbour for casting their eyes over the manuscript; Mark Beynon and the team at The History Press for doing such a sterling job; Alan Tomkins and Keith Hamshere for assistance with some of the photographs; Massimo Moretti at StudioCanal for permission to use *Ships with Wings* images; Barbara Broccoli, Michael G. Wilson and Meg Simmonds at Eon Productions; David Heyman and the *Harry Potter* team at Warner Bros.